An Insatiable First

An Insatiable First

190 Years of Shildon's Pioneering Railway Institute

David Reynolds

SHILDON RAILWAY
INSTITUTE

Dedicated to the Members of Shildon Railway Institute, past present and future. It is the people, not the buildings, that have always made the Institute what it is.

ACKNOWLEDGEMENTS
The author would like to thank the following for their kind assistance in providing information toward creating this history.

Cllr F. F. Bainbridge - whose 1933 Centenary Book was an invaluable source.

Roz Langley - for her memories throughout the years.

'Harry' Doughty - for the various artefacts shared with me.

Derek and Ann Walker - for their kind donation of the Jack Walker collection.

Val Bunting - for her memories.

ABOUT THE AUTHOR

Dave Reynolds was born in 1968 in Bishop Auckland. After a basic secondary education he attained a degree qualification in Design, and after a string of other jobs became a Business Analyst for a major UK telecommunications company. He has served as a Town Councillor, in Shildon not far from where he was born. He claims a life-long passion for history, for which he firmly blames his mother. This led him to become a founding Director of the Shildon Heritage Alliance CIC in 2019, and a champion for the Shildon Railway Institute, which was founded in 1833, becoming a world first. Dave's first book "The Wizard & The Typhoon," chronicling the lives of two Shildon born brass band composers, was published in 2022. In 2023 he was elected to the position of Chair of Shildon Railway Institute. When not knee-deep in history he's quite fond of gardening, allotment keeping and filmmaking.

Contents:

Foreword

28 November 2023 was the 190th Anniversary date of the founding of a society that would gradually become Shildon Railway Institute situated in the south of County Durham.

Why should this milestone warrant the creation of a book? Would it not be reasonable to wait until 2033 and create a bicentenary retrospective? This is a very fair question, and one that I will endeavour to answer.

There are many railway, and other industrial, institute buildings from the Georgian, Victorian or Edwardian eras scattered through the towns and villages of the United Kingdom. A few of these still fulfil the original purpose for which they were built. Many have been taken over and adapted, or converted, by a variety of businesses. Many stand empty or derelict. Many more have been lost to the wrecking ball as need for their facilities and services faded.

Shildon, as I write this, still has its Institute. Not only the Railway Institute building, but also the organisation occupying it, which, has operated in various capacities continuously throughout those nineteen decades. This is more important than readers might anticipate. Why? Because it is also a world first.

It was not the first industrial institute in the world. But it can, however, legitimately claim to be the first in the world to have been created for the benefit of, and purpose of improving the lives of, railway workers. Its mission within its community has evolved several times over nineteen decades, but it has still enjoyed one continuous thread of existence. Every Secretary of the committee has stepped into the shoes of the very first Secretary, the Stockton & Darlington Railway Company official Thomas MacNay.

This continued existence is a remarkable achievement, often in the face of adversity, and one worth being both proud and protective of. It is a living legacy of the founders of the town's railway industry, and of every generation of Shildonians since. It is a testimony to the will of the men and women who nurtured the seed of an idea, and then grew it through determination and hard work, to produce something community owned that still actively serves that community today. Yet there are many, living in the shadow of the most recent Institute building, or further afield, that don't know of, or understand, the amazing story of Shildon Railway Institute; why it came to be, or why it is still here as I write this. If the Institute is to continue, to evolve further, to serve and be passed on to the next generation, then this needs to change.

There is another, perhaps more important, reason why I have chosen to write a retrospective now, rather than in ten years time. This is that there is a very real likelihood that the organisation might not survive to reach its bicentenary. At the time of writing the hospitality sector, of which the Institute is nowadays considered to be a part, is under extreme financial pressure and Britain is losing clubs and pubs at a rapid rate. This has been the case for several years. Unless there is greater understanding and appreciation of why our ancient Institute is important enough to survive it may soon be gone forever.

The story of Shildon Railway Institute is the long story of the people of Shildon and their ongoing struggles to secure and maintain something of their very own. Something that was founded to meet their needs, forged from their endeavour, shaped by their culture and bound together by the threads of their collective experiences.

Put simply, Shildon Railway Institute is a cultural treasure, and unlike many that are usually found locked away or occasionally displayed behind glass, this is one which is still owned by its members, in which people can still immerse themselves and play a part in shaping to meet the needs of each generation. It is also a treasure without which we'd be a much poorer community. It may, through its constant evolution, no longer be fulfilling the exact purpose for which it was founded, but that same evolutionary process demonstrates its capability to continue that cycle of change enabling it to stay socially relevant now, and in the future.

I feel it important to acknowledge the contribution of Francis Frederick Bainbridge (1867-1957), who in 1933, produced the forerunner to this volume. This was a centenary retrospective of the Institute. Francis was a boilersmith and boiler inspector for the railway company, but also a Methodist preacher, avid historian, Institute member and local Justice of the Peace. The early part of my book draws considerably on his excellent work, mentioned later in this book, though I have added considerably to his account of those first 100 years.

I also want to apologise in advance for any inevitable omissions in this account of the Institute's history. There have been so many individual people responsible for driving and shaping it throughout these nineteen decades that it would take a huge volume to recognise all of their contributions. I am certain that readers will know of people in living memory whom they will feel should have been worthy of mention but whose individual contributions are not described here. It's important to consider that this book is a swift tour sweeping through a rich and busy history.

What is Shildon Railway Institute?

It is likely that many of you reading this live in or near Shildon, in which case what I am about to tell you may be deemed quite unnecessary. However I'll make provision for the fact that you, who are reading this, may not be familiar with the town.

Shildon is located in the south-west corner of County Durham, around twelve miles by road from Durham itself, and almost ten miles distance from the centre of Darlington, a town with whom its history is intrinsically linked. To the east of Shildon the countryside gently descends outward toward the mouth of the River Tees on the north-east coast of England, and to the west the landscape is more hilly and undulating in nature as you progress toward the Pennine Hills that make up the geographic spine running through the North of England.

If you've ever been to Shildon and driven up or down Redworth Road on the eastern side of town, you'd be forgiven for thinking that its Institute is the large building opposite the war memorial cross at New Shildon. You would only be partly correct.

It's true that by definition an institute can be an organisation, or the building that such an organisation operates from. For Shildon Railway Institute, it is both, and that is very important to understand. Take away either the organisation or the building and the Institute is devalued.

The Railway Institute at Shildon is a membership organisation. It can trace its roots almost to the beginnings of the settlement of New Shildon, once a town in its own right, it then being separated by acres of green fields from its neighbour Old Shildon on the hill above. This Institute was founded by prominent railwaymen on 28 November 1833, and as such is the oldest such Institute in the world to have been founded in connection with the railway industry. That fact makes it really quite unique.

That it has continued to serve the people of the community of Shildon right through to the present day is quite a remarkable achievement. Though its mission and organisational status have evolved several times throughout those 190 years, every joining member follows in the footsteps of generations of people from Shildon and the surrounding villages that became part of it before them. Every successive member of the Institute's management committee steps into the shoes of those first illustrious railwaymen who first had the vision to create something wonderful to serve their community. We'll explore the stories of some of those people in the pages that follow.

The purpose of this book is to tell the story of the Institute so far, in words and pictures, not only to mark its 190th year, but also to inspire members and non-members alike as we look ahead to the organisation's bicentenary in ten years time. It's a portrait of an extraordinary movement and its evolving place in the community over nineteen decades.

In Shildon Railway Institute, this community has a unique and socially valuable community owned and run organisation, and an asset that, if looked after and treated well, should continue to serve us well into the future. It is a living legacy the town has inherited that its first President, Timothy Hackworth, and his engineering companions would want us to take great care of, and pay forward to future generations.

The First Industrial Railway Town

Shildon is a relatively small town, with some ten-thousand residents, but one that proudly bears the honour of having a unique place in world history. If you have ever travelled anywhere in the world as a passenger on a train drawn by a locomotive, then the story of your journey starts right here in Shildon. It was the point of origin of the first steam hauled public railway journey in the world. It was not the birthplace of railways. Railways are a far older idea than we might think. The first known railway system is thought to have been one laid out by the ancient Babylonians over two millennia before the birth of Christ.

There is further evidence around Europe of other early railways of one form or another. One of the oldest being the Diolkos in Greece which ran between Schœnus and Lechæum and which involved grooved roads being used to move boats overland.

Gradually, engineers discovered that if a wagon is mounted upon rails, then a horse pulling it can tow a heavier load. It is mechanically more efficient. Nobody is quite sure about where the idea of these animal drawn wagon-ways originated, but early known examples include one used by German miners working in Cumbria in the 1560s. The evolution of these early rail systems appears to have been motivated by a need for industrial efficiency and to make supply of coal and minerals more profitable. Another example of an early rail based coal transportation system was one that was built at Prescot near Liverpool at the beginning of the seventeenth century. These early routes used rails of timber rather than the iron of later railways or the steel we associate with the industry today.

In the early 1670s, this technology moved closer to the kind of railway we recognise today when a new coal carrying railway was established at Tanfield. The new route, financed by a cluster of wealthy coal mine owning families that became known as the Grand Allies, was set up to transport coal from their various mines to coal staithes on the River Tyne. From there it could be transported by ship to the most profitable markets. The wagons would be hauled for many subsequent decades by horse and by rope before their eventual replacement by steam power. By the beginning of the nineteenth century, there were a number of private industrial railways across the North of England such as the railway systems at Wylam, Killingworth and Hetton.

The idea of transporting passengers on rails was a comparatively later one, due to its being far less profitable. Rail passenger transport was initially a by-product. It is thought that the first public railway to carry passengers was one set up in 1807, at a place called Oystermouth, by the Swansea and Mumbles Railway Company. Passengers were hauled along that route by horse, and the railway had been built primarily to transport coal, iron ore and limestone. This passenger service was merely an incidental opportunity to create a little additional revenue.

In 1802, an engineer named Richard Trevithick, seeking a way to harness the power of steam, created the first successful self-powered locomotive engine to transport a load along rails. Unsentimentally, he did not give this engine a name. It was only moderately successful but news travelled and gradually caught the imagination of other industrial engineers and inventors, triggering an exciting and innovative race to improve principles of steam locomotive power. A decade later, in 1812, the engineering partnership of John Blenkinsopp and Matthew Murray created a locomotive for the Middleton Railway, powered by steam and using driving cogs that connected with a toothed rail to provide forward and backward motion. This machine they named Salamanca.

A year later, three men collaborated on a locomotive for the owner of the Wylam Colliery on Tyneside. They were William Hedley, a colliery overseer, Jonathan Forster, an enginewright, and a young blacksmith named Timothy Hackworth who of course becomes an important figure in our story. Between them these three men designed and built Puffing Billy, in 1813, which is today the world's oldest surviving early steam locomotive. They followed this with a second locomotive named Wylam Dilly. Throughout the early years of these developments, all such innovations in steam rail power were intrinsically connected with heavy industry, and coal mining in particular. Much of the engineering work took place at the collieries themselves. Coal was the essential fuel necessary for the production of steam. It seems natural that this steam power it created should then be used to move vast quantities of that same coal to wherever it then needed to be taken.

Yet another Tyneside engineer, George Stephenson thought that he could improve upon the design of Puffing Billy, and so created his own first steam powered locomotive, Blucher, for the Killingworth Colliery in 1814. More Stephenson locomotives emerged at Killingworth in the years that followed. Stephenson was able to provide his son, Robert, with an education that led to his apprenticeship and the beginnings of his own route into locomotive engineering. It's certain that George Stephenson and Timothy Hackworth, who for a time worked for the Stephensons, were aware of each others respective advances and enhancements during this fascinating pioneering age.

Naturally, news of these technological advances travelled between the wealthy coal owners and investors of the North East of England, and the engineering feats achieved on Tyneside caught the attention of gentlemen considering whether to finance a new route to transport coal from the South-West Durham coalfield to the mouth of the River Tees.

This consortium of gentlemen, many from the Quaker community, had long been pondering how to solve the problem of getting coal from collieries at Witton Park to the coast quickly, cheaply and efficiently. The western section of the landscape to be traversed was especially challenging, due to its hilly nature. Once the first five miles of that journey had been passed, however, the terrain was a largely unobstructed gradual descent to the river mouth. The investors' first notion had been to investigate the viability of constructing a canal. In time however, their minds refocused upon mirroring, and exceeding, what rail transport had already achieved on Tyneside.

The leading Darlington based investor, Edward Pease, engaged George Stephenson to survey a route that improved upon one drafted by a Welshman, George Overton. Stephenson was chosen not specifically for his experience of building locomotive engines, but his overall experience of designing and engineering railway routes. His plan, which involved a combination of horse power and locomotive power, with two static steam engines to overcome the challenge of the two steepest hills, was found most agreeable to the investors. After some significant wrangling with landowners whose land would be crossed, an Act of Parliament was approved and work commenced on the Stockton & Darlington

14

Railway.

That the company adopted this name has long been a source of grievance for Shildonians, for it creates a popular perception that the route ran principally between the towns of Stockton and Darlington in much the same way as the later Liverpool & Manchester Railway connected those two cities. The name of the Stockton & Darlington Railway Company was chosen more in recognition that a large amount of the invested capital necessary to bring the project to fruition had been provided by financial backers residing in those two principal towns lying on the route. It is worth understanding though, that a further significant portion of the money was also invested by wealthy Quaker families in places further afield such as Whitby in North Yorkshire and beyond.

A great many books have been written about the origins of the Stockton and Darlington Railway, and how it came to be the first steam locomotive hauled public railway in the world. I do not intend to reproduce that story in any great detail here. It's simply important to know that the arrival of a railway at Shildon was the principal catalyst in the founding of a Railway Institute here. Lying toward the west end of this route, Shildon became the operational 'cradle' of the modern public steam hauled railway industry and the first of that railway company's important industrial railway towns.

Following a lengthy period of construction, in which bridges and support buildings were built, embankments raised, cuttings excavated and track bed laid, the Stockton and Darlington Railway opened with an inaugural journey on 27 September 1825. This was a journey that attracted a great deal of attention, and was well covered by the press at that time.

One of the most notable aspects was that after the train of coal chaldrons had been hauled over both the Etherley and Brusselton summits by the two powerful static steam engines there, it was then attached to a steam powered locomotive, designed and provided by Stephenson. Once attached, that locomotive pulled the coal all the way to the staithes at the mouth of the Tees. What a remarkable spectacle for those people who had gathered to watch, and doubly daring on account of the people that had clambered aboard to enjoy this remarkable journey.

Despite the success of the occasion, it would be a mistake to believe that the steam powered locomotives dominated operations on the line from that day forward. Much of the traffic along this 26 mile route was still drawn by horse, including the passenger traffic. The great locomotives were initially in short supply, and the Stephensons' early models suffered mechanical failures. Steam power was yet to be proven. There was a need for ongoing maintenance, and also to improve the technology. The materials and expertise for experimentation and development were expensive and for a number of years belief wavered. The future of steam power on the S&DR route hung in the balance.

The Stockton and Darlington Railway Company hired Timothy Hackworth who was by that time a relief manager at the Robert Stephenson & Co. factory, and one of the few men in the world with real experience of such engine building and operating a steam powered railway.

They had invited him Initially, in 1824, to build the static steam engines to power the Etherley and Brusselton inclines. Then in 1825 they offered him the post of resident engineer, supervisor and locomotive attendant. It proved to be an excellent choice. Hackworth applied himself to the challenges diligently. To him fell the task, not only to ensure that the locomotive traffic on the route continued to operate, but also that the static engines at Brusselton and Etherley continued to keep moving coal.

In order to carry out these duties this it was necessary to set up a base of operations in the vicinity, so the company erected a small and fairly mean workshop for him and his small team of engineers as well as a few basic houses. From this seed, a whole new industrial town gradually germinated.

Being in the shadow of the old market town of Shildon up on the hill, this new place acquired the name of New Shildon, with the more senior of the two towns adopting the prefix 'Old'.

It was Hackworth's innovative endeavours in the town that not only went on to ensure that his name would be forever revered in Shildon, but which also would finally settle the argument over whether steam power was superior to, and could be more efficient than, the horse. It seems almost unbelievable now, given how steam power developed afterward, to think that during those first five years it was still cheaper, and therefore more financially efficient, to pull the coal using horses.

A number of 'improved' locomotives had been added to the company's stock between 1825 and 1827, all of which continued to be outperformed by horses on the line. This changed in 1827, when Hackworth as locomotive superintendent, placed a new locomotive of his own design on the line. This was the six wheeled locomotive "Royal George". It incorporated a blast pipe that would divert steam into the chimney forcing the exhaust fumes to leave the engine faster and thus drawing more air into the furnace to make the coal hotter, thereby producing more steam power. It was a complete game-changer.

The resulting reduction in operating costs, and impressive profits reported to the company, settled the argument. By April

1833 the company was able to mandate the removal of horses from the line east of New Shildon altogether. To make this possible it was clear to the company that they would need more locomotives like "Royal George," and an engineering works to build some of them. The workforce expanded and, where once there had only been a rural population of eleven to thirteen people, a booming town was born.

The new town was built upon land that fell within the catchment of two townships. The township of Shildon, which in medieval times had been held by the Belasyse family, and the township of Thickley Punchardon, part of the medieval land holdings of the Lilburne family. It was mainly agricultural land, some of which was quite waterlogged. Before the Stockton and Darlington Railway Company would agree to purchase the portion of land for their works and railway sidings at New Shildon, they required that the owner of the land, Sir Philip Christopher Musgrave, must first drain it.

Timothy Hackworth was, of course, one of the first residents of New Shildon. He lived in one of five cottages adjacent to the infant works, which in 1825 consisted of a blacksmith's shop and a shed for two engines. This was not the house that we associate with Hackworth today. The workshop was nothing more than a narrow barn-style building. The resident blacksmith was Thomas Dobson, who had two or three assistants. The resident foreman joiner, for the joinery work that was necessary, was Thomas Coulson. That workshop gradually grew, but in addition, from 1833, and despite still being in the employment of the S&DR, Hackworth also built his own second private engineering works at New Shildon, which he called the Soho Works.

It wasn't just the railway work that drew people to the fledgling town. A number of supporting industries sprang up quickly, including quarries, brick and tile works and lime kilns, all of which required workers. Additionally local explorations in search of more precious coal bore fruit, and the Pease family, who had been so instrumental in the creation of the railway, opened Adelaide Colliery in 1830, which continued to generate wealth for them until it closed in 1925. Shildon Lodge Colliery, Copy Crooks Colliery and the Black Boy Colliery at Eldon all opened within a few years of each other, placing more coal on the S&DR line. Additionally, up in the older Shildon, a useful brass and iron foundry was established.

When the works at New Shildon started there were only 20 people working under Timothy Hackworth's supervision. By 1827 when the "Royal George" was built there were fifty persons working at the works. A description of New Shildon in 1834 noted that public houses, shops and other businesses were growing in number. By 1841 there were 452 residents.

The early parts of this new town were the streets that are almost forgotten and irrelevant today. They were Chapel Street where the first of the town's Methodist Chapels was erected in 1831, Adelaide Street and Strand Street, and of these very little remains of any original buildings. Back then, they formed the residential core. There were some buildings on what later became Byerley and Redworth Roads which were bisected by the railway line. There were also Richmond Street, Railway Terrace, Temperance Street, Station Street, Mechanic Street and Mill Street, with a steam corn mill at its northern end. These were all added as demand for accommodation grew.

Some, but not all, early railway employees at Shildon were unable to write even their own names, and of course, this being a brand new industry, many had no previous experience in engine work and were to some extent initially unskilled. Of course they would have been selected for having some aptitude or otherwise suitable qualities, but many workers were far from being the finished article. The working conditions were equally crude. In his book celebrating the Centenary of the Railway Institute in 1933, the writer Councillor Francis Frederick Bainbridge sets the following scene:

> "There were only hand lathes on the premises, there was no turn table, no means of raising heavy parts but by ropes and pulleys, and no appliance for lifting engines or boilers but the screw jack of ancient design with four 'horns,'— to which a lever was attached to work the jack. Boilers and cylinders were obtained from Newcastle, and wheels — then of metal and often lasting only about a month — procured from Bradford and other towns. An old workman has narrated that during the building of the "Royal George" Mr Hackworth would be at work on the engine by the flickering light of a candle in weather frosty enough to freeze the tallow as it began to run down the candle sides."

The houses where the railway workers and others lived are understood to have been quite mean. They may have been newly built but they were scantily furnished and not provided with fresh running water. It would be 1868 before the Shildon and Weardale Water Company, another venture in which the Pease family held a significant stake, brought a clean water supply to the town. The streets were referred to as being a quagmire in winter or after a shower of rain. Sanitation was no worse than elsewhere, but with natural watercourses being used for sewage it is understood that there were some devastating epidemics in the early years.

A chapel had been built for the spiritual and moral benefit of the Wesleyan Methodists, and that project had been championed by Hackworth himself. It incorporated a school room to provide some religious education for the new community's youngest residents. It was built directly adjacent to the Globe Inn, which along with the Masons Arms were some of the earliest public houses in the area. As you might expect, the Methodists and the publican were hardly likely to make ideal neighbours, and we are told that the landlord would try to annoy the preacher and worshippers next door by beating tin cans and occasionally offering vocal accompaniment.

A Library for the Promotion of Useful Knowledge

As well as the blacksmiths, joiners and mechanics at the works, there were of course a number of locomotive drivers and firemen, or "engine feeders" as they were quaintly known, resident in the town. This was because the majority of the fleet of S&DR locomotives were kept at New Shildon, close to the works. These men, being in an occupation that was considered particularly skilful, were also particularly well paid. They found the Globe Inn a useful and popular place to spend their excess wages.

A particular incident that took place here appears to have been a factor instrumental in the idea of founding an Institute. Councillor Bainbridge relates it in the Institute's centenary retrospective as follows:

> "Mr John Graham has recorded that one evening when passing the end of Chapel Street he was arrested by a tremendous noise coming form the vicinity of the Globe Inn, and thinking that nothing less than a riot had broken out, hastened to ascertain the cause of the uproar. With much difficulty he gained an entrance into the inn, when to his surprise and disgust he found that some of the engine drivers had placed their watches in a frying pan which was placed on the fire, and were betting as to whose watch would be the first to stop."

John Graham, had been born in 1799, so would have been in his early thirties at the time of this incident. He had been raised as an orphan and sent to work at Hetton Colliery, probably as a boy trapper, sitting in darkness opening and closing ventilation traps to allow the coal tubs to pass through. After dislocating his ankle in an accident he attended a day school, and continued his education in the evenings. He became a coal hewer, and then worked his way up such that by 1822 he was Head Underground Overlooker.

When the Stockton and Darlington Railway were looking for a Traffic Manager to manage the coal and mineral traffic, John Graham applied and, from a short list of 52 applicants, was chosen for the post. That he had not done the job previously would not have been so much of a barrier as this was an emerging industry. Graham, having risen from humble origins to a position of some responsibility, understood the value of applying oneself to acquiring some education, and in maintaining a clear mind.

Above: The Congregational Church on Chapel Street, New Shildon. The gap between buildings to the right is the site of the Globe Inn which was site of the first meeting to establish what was initially a library but which evolved to become the Institute.

Part of John Graham's day to day job was to ensure the application of discipline upon operations along the railway route, and it is probably due to this that the incident concerning frying pocket watches was recorded. Graham kept journals describing incidents of indiscipline, which he then reported upward to the railway company's management. Though many of the operators pulling coal and passengers on the line were acting privately, they were expected to adhere to rules and regulations set by the company, and the company were able to impose fines. Many of the incidents recorded relate to laziness, confrontations between traffic meeting each other on the line and operating in a state of drunkenness. He must have considered that were he able to positively influence the intellectual and moral qualities of railway workers it ought, if nothing else, to reduce occurrences of such unwanted behaviour.

It was suggested that senior figures meet to exchange ideas on what could be done. The meeting took place on Thursday 28 November, a little ironically in the cellar of the Globe Inn, the place where the pocket watch incident had taken place. We are told that this very first meeting involved John Graham himself, Timothy Hackworth, John Glass, John Pickering, Thomas MacNay, and several others with a practical interest in the matter. Among the latter were John Hallam, John Atkinson, Anthony Hodgson, J Stabler, J Woodman, F Cockshott, R Elliott, E Humble and John Luke.

During the ensuing discussion, a proposal was made, which was the founding of an institution for the betterment of the local workforce, and that this would be a membership society with a library which would be made available to members on a subscription basis. The subscriptions would enable the growth of the organisation, the acquisition of new reading materials and the engagement of guest speakers. This would subsequently be advertised and promoted to the residents of New Shildon.

Timothy Hackworth was elected to be its first President. Thomas MacNay, would be its Secretary. The latter quickly set about creating a constitution for the new institution. Every President and Secretary since has experienced the privilege of stepping into the shoes of these two very distinguished men, and continuing their legacy for both town and people.

The society secured the patronage of Joseph Pease, who was not only an influential figure in both management and ownership of the Stockton and Darlington Railway but also a sitting Member of Parliament. Other early supporters were Francis Mewburn, solicitor for the railway company, Josiah Smithson and Colonel Henry Stobart, both board members of railway company.

The latter of these two was also the proprietor of Etherley Colliery. These were four men of significant means and influence.

According to John Glass, in his speech at the Institute's Anniversary Dinner in September 1863, the prospectus for the Institute, drafted by Thomas MacNay contained the following opening words:

> "Shildon Library for the Promotion of Useful Knowledge. The founders of this Institute being deeply impressed with the numerous advantages to be derived from learning, have been induced to establish a library for the benefit of the inhabitants of Shildon and its vicinity, hoping that, through the books connected therewith and the lectures that may be delivered, useful knowledge may be extensively disseminated and perpetuated to generations yet unborn."

Above: George Graham, Traffic Manager of the Stockton and Darlington Railway, whose encounter with locomotive drivers gambling reportedly inspired the founding of the Institute.
From a portrait once held at the Institute.

This first meeting of the founders was reported in two newspapers. The first, the Durham County Advertiser of Friday 6 December 1833 stated that the institution was a "Library for the Promotion of Useful Knowledge" and said that "a very favourable report of the Institution, which produced cheering anticipations of its future success, was read." The Newcastle Courant followed up with a very similar report the following day.

And so, through the foresight and ambition of these canny railwaymen, seeking to improve the prospects and suitability of their employees, the first such organisation to be founded in connection with the railway industry was born.

It's worth noting that it wasn't called Shildon Railway Institute from the beginning. The society, that germinated from the seed planted on that Thursday evening in November 1833, underwent several evolutionary stages throughout the decades of its existence, following societal trends and the evolving needs of its members. It took a few wise heads to recognise the need for such an institution. Had the same men instead asked the engine drivers and firemen what they felt they needed at that meeting, they might well have responded by requesting more pocket watches and frying pans.

That the institution was originally named a "Library for the Promotion of Useful Knowledge" is interesting, and may well be related to interests of its first patron. Joseph Pease had been elected as Member of Parliament for South Durham only a year earlier. He was the first Quaker permitted to serve as an MP. A requirement to take an oath of office had proven a barrier to other Quakers before him. Fortuitously for Pease, a decision by a Special Committee permitted him to 'affirm' rather than 'swear' his oath upon taking his seat in Parliament. As a Quaker he also refused to observe the Parliamentary tradition of removing his hat when entering the House of Commons.

Pease was by nature a Whig, and his Parliamentary business would have taken him regularly to London where he would have met Lord Henry Brougham, a Whig peer who had previously served as MP for Camelford, Winchelsea and Knaresborough in that order. Like Joseph Pease, Brougham took an interest in education. In 1826 he had been instrumental in the forming of the Society for the Diffusion of Useful Knowledge, a Whig organisation that published books targeted at people who were unable to access formal teaching, or who preferred self education. The publications were intended to give the working, and middle, classes more advanced educational material than they would otherwise be able to afford. They selected the information to distribute and made sure that the printing costs were sufficiently low as to make it affordable.

So if Brougham's organisation was set up for the 'diffusion' of such knowledge, we can reasonably theorise, that his fellow Whig, Joseph Pease's complimentary new society and library in New Shildon might be intended to play a part in 'promoting' it.

Brougham's society continued through till 1846, by which time the Institute at New Shildon had chosen to alter its title to become one of the Mechanics Institutes that were springing up around the country. Despite this and other later changes of name or organisational format it remained the same organisation, with one continuous committee system, and is still the first such to have been founded in connection with the railway industry anywhere in the world.

Thomas MacNay, the first Secretary

Thomas MacNay was one of the most significant working figures in the operation of the Stockton & Darlington Railway Company. He was born at Wallsend on 2 July 1810. His working career began in 1819 when he was engaged at the offices of Messrs Hawthorn and Co., engine builders, at their Newcastle works. As a young man in 1831, he was engaged by Colonel Stobart and Joseph Pease, on behalf of the Stockton & Darlington Railway Company, in connection with Hackworth's engine works at New Shildon. Initially he was taken on as a store-man, but graduated to become a draughtsman, and then an accountant. He spent several years in New Shildon, where he reportedly invested a great deal of time in developing the Sunday School, and it was here, of course, that he became involved in the founding of the library that became today's Institute, and set out its manifesto which we quoted earlier.

Having made such a promising impression, he moved to Darlington in 1838, was eventually appointed in 1849 to the post of Secretary of the S&DR. Once there he, in 1858, established a similar library to the one he co-founded at Shildon. He served as President there and much more besides. An obituary following his death explained that he frequently not only took the chair and directed the executive, but also from time to time gave practical statistical lectures. These included one on 'England's Progress' in November 1858, and 'Our Roads and Railways,' two years later. The second of these two highly regarded lectures was printed, published and distributed. It was said that no man in the locality was a greater authority on the metallurgy of the district, and in November 1855, he delivered an interesting lecture to the Mechanics' Institution at Wolsingham, on 'Iron, its Manufacture, and the Trade Generally'. Another notable lecture was on the subject of 'Prophecy' wherein he expressed the power of statistics and data in predicting what may come, a principle many business leaders today would be most familiar with.

Above: Thomas MacNay, S&DR employee, first Secretary of the Institute and author of its original manifesto.
From a portrait once held at the Institute.

MacNay was considered to be a "self made man" and was largely self-educated too, with a reputation for overworking and rarely giving himself any respite. It is thought that in some ways this diligence may have contributed to the decline of his health. On 12 May 1868, his youngest son died, and it is believed that this affected him quite profoundly. From that date his own health began a gradual and perceptible decline to the point that more and more of his work was devolved to his son John Edward MacNay, the assistant-secretary of the S&DR, who had himself been employed by the company for twenty years by the time Thomas died.

At other stages in his career, Thomas MacNay had been secretary of the Auckland and Weardale, Wear Valley, and Middlesborough and Redcar subsidiary branches of the railway company, striving to find ways to return those routes to strong revenue generation for the shareholders whenever their profitability placed their viability in jeopardy.

He was an active promoter of the Darlington and Barnard Castle Railway, the Middlesborough and Guisborough Line, the South Durham and Lancashire Union and Eden Valley Railways, and strove to keep them profitable ahead of their later merger into the North Eastern Railway.

Following an accident in 1861, which involved a special train commissioned by the Darlington Mechanics Institute to take them to Windermere, MacNay had been impressed by the 'block system' for railway signalling in managing traffic along the line, and persisted in efforts to apply it wherever feasible and practicable, especially where the train traffic was heaviest and most dangerous. The system effectively prevented two trains from entering the same section of the line at any one time. In addition, he also found time to serve as a councillor for the North Ward of Darlington in his later years.

Thomas passed away at his home, Brookside, Darlington at noon on Saturday 6 August 1869, with the cause of his death being cancer in the stomach, complicated by additional issues relating to his kidneys. He was survived by his wife, four sons and three daughters. As a later mark of respect, a street in the North Road area of Darlington, was named after him.

No Room at the Inn

Any visitor to today's Railway Institute building, on Shildon's Redworth Road, might assume that this oldest of railway institutions had always had the benefit of a grand building in which to conduct its affairs. The reality, however, is that for the first twenty-seven years of its existence it merely occupied space on the premises of other organisations.

After forming its first committee, the society reached out to the public houses of New Shildon to ask for a room to act as a reading room in which to host their library and provide space for occasional lectures. The Globe Inn could not spare space for this purpose, nor could the Black Bull which once stood at corner of the junction between Adelaide Street and Byerley Road. The Masons Arms had initially had space to spare, but this had since been requisitioned by the railway company as a station and booking office for passenger traffic travelling over the rope hauled Brusselton incline to West Auckland, as well as a railway directors committee room. Daniel Adamson's Grey Horse Inn, a short distance away at the fringe of Old Shildon, was by that time doubling up as a goods station.

The only available solution was to strike a deal with the Wesleyan schoolroom which was attached to the Methodist chapel on Chapel Street. Through the intervention of Timothy Hackworth arrangements were made to make this available at times when it was not not being used for its primary purpose.

Despite the kind co-operation of the Methodists in this benign partnership, the new institution was not entirely satisfied with sharing premises. The arrangement was too restrictive on when the members of the library could access its collection. It remained an ambition from the outset that the organisation should somehow seek premises of its own. The hours in which the railwaymen were not at their labours frequently coincided with times when the Methodists, often the same people, wanted to use the Wesleyan schoolroom for church purposes, leading to conflicts.

In his retrospective history of the first hundred years of the Institute, Francis Bainbridge hypothesises imagining the keen interest taken by the residents of New Shildon, and also those people of the surrounding district. From what I have gleaned from the organisation's early report books I'm not so sure that there was quite so much enthusiasm in the community, and it's likely that a great deal of promotion and hard work would have been required to build up a membership.

The library itself had a very modest beginning, comprising a mere handful of books. We know something about the books from surviving catalogues of their titles, and perhaps surprisingly they were not all on subjects of science, technology, mechanics, spiritual enrichment and character building. Many focused on history, myths, legends or foreign travel. It seems that a broad spectrum of subjects was made available, perhaps even with the intention of simply encouraging members to read in the hope that they would absorb a range of information.

Information telling us about about the earliest years of the new institution is very rare. The National Archives at Kew in London hold several documents and record books relating to the first century of the organisation, but nothing held there is older than a library record book that commences from 1842. However, in 2023, Shildon Railway Institute received a very special gift from a surprising source, which reveals something about how the Library for the promotion of Useful Knowledge was operated.

The gift was presented by Derek Walker and his wife, Anne. Derek's father, Jack, had been a railway employee, working for a time at the goods depot in Bishop Auckland and later at several railway stations in the area including the one at Hunwick. Jack had amassed a collection of railway artefacts spanning the early years of the region's steam railway industry. The oldest item in that collection was a single piece of lined paper that contains stunning evidence of how the library operated.

The sheet lists the names of several of the members starting with Timothy Hackworth as member number one, Thomas MacNay as member number two and going on to list a further twenty-three names, several of which went on to play a significant part in the development of the Institute at New Shildon. It was thought by the Walker family for several years for that the list was the very first members list, but closer inspection reveals that the list is from 1837, rather than 1833 when the Library was founded. The paper on which the information is written has a watermark which reads "1835". Nonetheless this small piece of paper tells us a lot about how the Library was operated. There are columns across the page headed with dates from mid-October through to early December of 1837. The dates given all correspond to Thursdays - which tells us that this was the evening upon which the members of the Library attended the Wesleyan Schoolroom to meet. There each member would return the book that they had borrowed at the previous meeting. The books were all numbered, and the number from whichever book had been borrowed at a meeting was recorded against that member in the corresponding date column. As each book was brought back to the Library at the following session the number was crossed out to mark that it had been returned. Each member was only permitted to take one book at a time, a rule replicated when a further sister-library was opened in Darlington many years later in 1858. Another learning from this important piece of historical evidence is that even in its earliest days membership of the Library was not restricted to railway employees. Though many were indeed engine fitters, blacksmiths or enginemen, several early members had other occupations. For example, William Cleminson was a stone merchant, Thomas Cree a shoe maker, George Forster a brick maker and Chris Applegarth a grocer. This openness regarding who could and could not be a member should not be surprising news. It was a policy adopted throughout the lifetime of the various phases of the Institute. Even during the period during which it was under the patronage of the British Rail Staff Association there were times when membership was open to a limited number of applicants other than railway employees and their families.

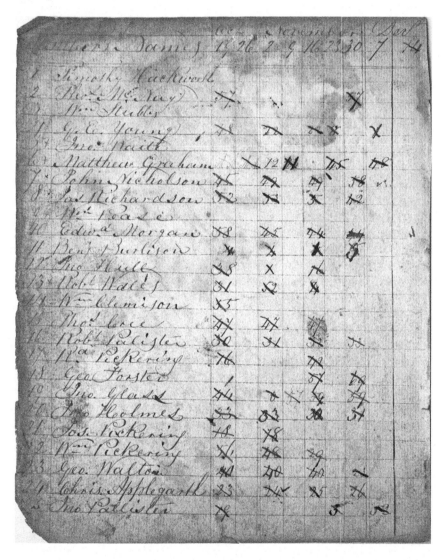

Above: Image of the list of members for October to December 1837 showing which book they had borrowed each week. Timothy Hackworth is listed as member number one. From the Institute's 'Jack Walker Collection'.

For many poorer working men of New Shildon, the first challenge in taking advantage of the new Institute's services might have been gaining the necessary reading skills. A national report on literacy commissioned in 1840 suggested that sixty-seven percent of men and fifty-one percent of women were to some degree literate, though it's a little unclear what qualified as literate for this report. It's also possible that those who joined the society in the early days may well have found their enthusiasm rewarded not only with the acquisition of new and useful knowledge, but also with the favour of the society's senior officers, who would also have influence over one's progression in the workplace. As we will see, many of the members from the early years did go on to enjoy distinguished careers, and not all of those were in the field of railway engineering or operation. Institute reports from the mid-1850s, however, suggest that the committee felt that there were still many who might benefit from joining that had not yet taken the opportunity to subscribe.

Concerning the acquisition of books, the society was partly dependent upon philanthropists, patrons and other kindly donors. Very few people in the surrounding community would have been in possession of the kinds of books desired so as to be able to donate them, and the organisation itself otherwise had only the subscription money from members to buy them. Despite this, the committee, and patrons, committed to making it a successful venture, and excelled in putting their influence to work to secure a substantial number of volumes for the collection. In Bainbridge's history he acknowledges that at several points in its history the Institute would have floundered without the patronage of the railway various companies acting as benefactors.

As the collection of books, and the membership, gradually grew, it became increasingly apparent that the Institute was encroaching more and more upon the operation of the Wesleyan schoolroom and that the situation was becoming unsustainable. An opportunity to meet the demand for a dedicated reading room arose in 1842, when the Institute was already almost a decade old.

The success of the Stockton and Darlington Railway, and the discovery of even more coal and mineral deposits to the west of Shildon, increased the imperative to lay down more branch lines west of Shildon. Yet the geographical barrier of the hill upon which Old Shildon stood remained a challenge to transporting minerals and goods from that region. The rope hauled inclines, operating at their maximum efficiency, could not handle any more traffic.

The answer was to dig a tunnel right under the hill so that locomotives and wagons could pass directly under Old Shildon. Consequently the Shildon Tunnel Company was founded.

It was once again an ambitious project for the Stockton & Darlington Railway Company, being the first proposal to excavate a railway tunnel beneath an urban settlement anywhere in the world. By 1839 the company secretary, Mr Barnard, placed an appeal in the Durham County Advertiser for excavators, masons and contractors to view the plans for the tunnel at the S&DR offices in Darlington, and to submit their tenders to the company's Chief Engineer, John Harris.

Above: The Prince of Wales Tunnel at Shildon opened in 1842 and was the world's first railway tunnel to be excavated beneath an urban settlement. Its opening enabled the Institute to open a reading room at the Masons Arms in space previously used as a ticket office and waiting room.

This 1300 yard long tunnel, formally known as the Prince of Wales Tunnel, with its seven vertical ventilation shafts, took around three years to plan, excavate and construct, and was ready for the final brick, the keystone on its entrance arch, to be placed on 10 January 1842. It opened on 18 April that year, with the moment being marked by a coach containing directors and friends being drawn through it by locomotive, followed by another with general passengers being drawn through by horse. To get an understanding of the significance of the impact of this tunnel one need look no further than an article in the London Sun on Friday 22 April 1842 which explained that:

"The tunnel is above a mile long, and passengers can now be conveyed from London to South Church station by railway; thence to Rainton Meadows by omnibuses, when they will again be conveyed to Newcastle by railway, so that the entire distance from London to Newcastle may be traversed by railway, with the exception of the one-and-a-half hour's travelling on the road between South Church and Rainton Meadows."

Who today would ever have thought that passengers would have found the route from Darlington through Shildon to South Church so convenient in finding their way from London to Newcastle?

This new route between Shildon and West Auckland meant that there was no longer a need for passengers to travel over the Brusselton Incline to West Auckland. They could now climb into carriages to be transported by locomotive power straight through the hill that had for so long been a land barrier. As a consequence, the temporary booking office at the Masons' Arms was no longer required. A new station was built to serve Shildon, the third to be brought into service in fifteen years.

This redundant space at the Masons Arms was an ideal size to serve as a reading room for the Institute. It was still practically new and centrally located in the town. It had become the practice of the Institute committee to produce a written half-yearly report every six months, relating the state of the organisation to members. The Institute's half-yearly report from 31 December 1842 captured the intent of the committee as regards the reading room:

"In their labours your committee has not lost sight of what has been generally considered as a necessary auxiliary to institutions of this nature, viz:- a Reading Room, and they are happy to inform you that there is every prospect of a commodious and suitable one being obtained in the course of three months. At the same time they deem it their duty to remark that they do not expect it to be carried on by gratuitous labour, also a regular expenditure must take place in order to secure all the advantages which may be derived from it.

We do not see much difficulty on this point, as no doubt the members will heartily respond to any call which may be made, whether in the shape of donations, or a small increase in the regular subscriptions. The latter method seems to us to be the most feasible."

Becoming a Mechanics Institute

By this point the organisation was formally referring to itself as a Mechanics Institute, making it part of yet another social movement of the early industrial age. We believe that this transition to a Mechanics Institute took place at the beginning of the 1840s. A library record book for the New Shildon Mechanics Institute exists at the National Archives in Kew and it commences from 1842 which coincides approximately with the opening of the Prince of Wales Tunnel. It was a key year for the organisation.

The Mechanics Institute movement has its origins in the work of George Birkbeck, who was born in 1776 and was a physician, academic, philanthropist and pioneer in adult education. Birkbeck was disposed to offering free annual lectures. Originally based in London, he left there in 1804 for Edinburgh where in 1821 he established the first of his Mechanics Institutes. That Institute commenced with a lecture on Chemistry and was soon subscribed to by over 450 men each paying a quarterly subscription fee. The idea was to attract working men, specifically civil and mechanical engineers, and to provide them with technical and scientific education. With the Industrial Revolution having produced a new class of reader at the end of the 18th century, this movement grew with gusto, and similar institutions were founded in major centres across the United Kingdom as well as the wider British Empire. In Australia, for example, institutes were initially founded in Hobart, Melbourne and Sydney.

This young and dynamic movement was a perfect fit for the Institute at Shildon, which was still employing men at the cutting edge of mechanical and civil engineering. The Shildon engineers weren't just building the wagons essential to transporting good sand raw materials. They were also designing and building ever improving, and ever more powerful, locomotive engines. In addition, Hackworth was also developing engines and machinery for other industries, from maritime shipbuilding to brewing. It would seem to be a natural progression for the "Library for Promotion of

Useful Knowledge" to take that next evolutionary step to become a Mechanics Institute.

We must be clear here in establishing that the New Shildon Mechanics Institute was not the first Mechanics Institute in the world, but it didn't need to be to remain of unique significance. It already held the distinction of being the first organisation created for railway engineers. It simply suited the organisation to change direction slightly that time. It was yet another cycle of evolution.

Moving in to a New Home

The Institute formed a sub-committee to manage the process of moving into the new Reading Room at the Masons Arms, for which the organisation agreed that it would pay a yearly rent to the railway company who owned the building. That sub-committee reported its progress to the wider body of members.

Above: The former Masons Arms public house (not the original building) where the Institute moved into its first dedicated reading room in 1842.

Furniture was obtained, including two tables manufactured from deal, with matching benches, purchased from a Mr Braithwaite for the sum of two guineas. The railway company, for their part, provided a large cupboard especially manufactured to hold the library books. A number of members of the committee contributed toward the cost of a chandelier to be hung in the room which would provide enough light for reading. Hat pegs were also erected, so that the 'gentlemen' might hang up their hats. Members in the early years were predominantly, if not exclusively, male.

Other gentlemen supporters of the Institute donated additional items to make the room comfortable. William Kitchen of Darlington provided a fender for the fireplace and set of fire-irons. T Hines provided roller blind fittings and both William Bouch and R Corner offered blind rollers and blinds. A small number of cash donations were also offered.

The securing of a permanent premises necessitated the production of a new set of rules for the use and governance of this reading room, and the sub-committee wasted no time in drafting them, presenting them to the main committee to be approved. Additionally a first caretaker, Mr Hamilton, was appointed on a salary of £8 a year.

With all the essential details and furnishings settled, the Institute held an opening event for the reading room in April 1843. Having this private space lifted its appeal significantly, resulting in more people opting to join. The half-yearly report by the Institute's committee in the summer of 1843 explained that the membership had swollen from 66 persons to 122, and went on to explain that the gain was "four times as many as were added on any previous half year". This shows, as we had earlier supposed, that the Institute had been initially had quite a low membership. The acquisition of a dedicated reading room was the beginning of a new and more promising era. It also marked the end of the period during which members were limited to meeting only on a Thursday evening. Now they had access to a place where they could potentially come and go as they pleased, and stay as long as they wished. The opening hours could be defined by the committee. Though they are not recorded anywhere we have yet seen, they are quite likely to have been similar to those of the later Darlington reading room and library, which was open daily, except on Sundays, with the reading room being open between noon and two-o'clock in the afternoon, and again at half-past-four until half-past-nine. The library, which had to be attended by a Librarian, was open between six and eight in the evening.

The new intake of members being keen to use the new reading room was hardly surprising given that homes in New Shildon at the time were small in size and contained large families. Evidence in the 1841 census shows households of nine, ten or eleven people were not uncommon. The opportunity to spend time in the calm sanctuary of the reading room will have made it an appealing retreat.

Education, Education, Education

As we advanced through the decades of the nineteenth century there was in increased emphasis placed on the need for education of poorer children and working people. Initially this was either a religious, philanthropic or economic consideration, but by 1833 even the Government felt the need to support educational movements, offering sums of money for the construction of schools. New Shildon was no exception.

In 1841 the Stockton and Darlington Railway Company erected a British School building on Station Street. Unsurprisingly the motivation for doing so again had its roots in the Quaker movement dear to the hearts of that company's directorship.

British Schools were a concept devised by a Quaker named Joseph Lancaster, who had become concerned in the late eighteenth century that the poorer classes were being denied the opportunity of an education. He understood that the main cost of tutelage centred on the need to pay teachers a salary. He consequently developed a method of teaching whereby a single teacher could be responsible for educating 300 or more boys, all accommodated in one large school room. This was to be precisely the format of the British School building at New Shildon. The school building still stands today, its one large hall proving ideal in the building's most recent use as a dance school.

That system of having only one principal teacher was enabled by having older more able children, who had already received some education, teach what they had learned down-over to the younger children. This provided a cheap basic education with limited resources. The curriculum provided was little more than 'the three Rs'; reading, writing and arithmetic. Some schools at this time occasionally added in a little history, geography and grammar, and there was likely to have been an element of Bible reading.

It may seem strange now, but there were many at the time who objected to educating the working classes, and who felt that children were being educated above their station. Some in the higher echelons of early Victorian society seemed quite comfortable with the stratification of society and lack of social mobility. Yet social mobility was possible, even within the lowest class in that society where there were sub-strata from the labouring working men, through skilled artisans to the poorer educated men. It was possible for men born in low circumstances to elevate themselves, as George Stephenson and Timothy Hackworth had done.

Requiring a schoolmaster, the railway company appointed Mr John Pickering, who was a young mechanic at the Shildon Engine Works. John had been born in Bishopwearmouth, Sunderland, and like many others in New Shildon at the time, had moved to this area for the opportunity to work in the new industry.

A committee of railway officials and employees governed the new school, and every railway employee in the area paid one penny per week from their wages towards the school's expenses. Additionally those parents that sent their children to the school paid a penny per week per child. This was in accordance with a charging system adopted by British Schools nationwide.

To show that it was never too late to learn, adults were offered evening classes; an opportunity in which the committee of the Institute had great belief. The securing of a permanent venue opened the doorway to the Institute partnering with the school to offer such services to the community. Throughout the sixty years between 1843 and the passing of the Education Act of 1902, the New Shildon Mechanics Institute became the main provider of adult evening classes in the town. The objective was to provide a range of tuition that combined elementary and technical education. This curriculum was complemented by a series of public lectures on various subjects. We'll take a closer look at some of the lectures later.

Seeing the potential of the education that the Institute could now provide, the committee wrote in their end of year report for December 1843 that:

"The subject of classes for evening instruction has claimed the close attention, and three have been established which so far have worked well, and bid for to prove a benefit to both the village and the Institute."

To provide these evening classes, it was necessary to identify suitable tutors. Three suitable men put themselves forward to offer their services without charging the Institute for their time. The first was thirty-year-old William Bouch, the second, a Quaker, Edgar Gilkes who would go on to employ men at his iron foundry, and the last Robert Rowland.

The success of this programme of education, combined with the availability of suitable literature at the Institute, appears to have been influential in the subsequent success of several early members of the Institute who went on to become prominent in engineering and other technical and social fields. We will take a look at some of these people in future chapters.

Despite the Institute now having its own leased premises, the accommodation was still quite small and, though well suited to be a reading room, was too small for other purposes. Arrangements were thus made with the governing board of the British School Room so that it became the venue for larger meetings of the Institute membership. Half-yearly meetings of the Institute membership and some of the educational lectures were hosted there.

William Bouch (1813-1876)

William Bouch, a figure of some significance in Shildon's industrial history, had been born in Thursby, Cumbria in 1813. He was the son of a retired sea captain and publican. As a young man he had become apprenticed to Robert Stephenson & Co, before becoming the Chief Engineer of Butterley Iron Works in Derbyshire. Whilst engaged in that latter role he travelled to Russia along with a ship load of machinery for the Black Sea Navigation Company. There he was briefly appointed Chief Engineer of a Russian Navy vessel.

He subsequently was appointed Locomotive Engineer of the Stockton & Darlington Railway, and took on the management of the company's Shildon Works in 1840 after Timothy Hackworth had diverted his attention fully to his own Soho Works. Bouch was thus believed to be well equipped to provide a technical education to the aspiring young men of New Shildon. As part of his role for the railway company William designed locomotives, and in 1860, around two decades after becoming involved with the Institute, William would design the first British locomotives to use the successful American locomotive wheel pattern of 4-4-0.

He also invented a feedwater heater which earned the nickname "Bouch's Coffee Can". This was a water sleeve around the locomotive's chimney pre-heating the water before it was fed to the locomotive's boiler. Other patented inventions from his time at Shildon Works include the "radial screw reversing gear," which he introduced in 1865; the "steam retarder'" designed to bring a brake power to bear on cylinder pistons and also a rail mounted crane with shear stabilising legs for the recovery of derailed locomotives and rolling stock.

Above: William Bouch, locomotive designer and manager of the S&DR's Shildon Works. Bouch gave tuition at the Institute and served for a time as Treasurer. From a portrait once held at the Institute.

Bouch was instrumental in the design of the long-boiler locomotives that would become employed on the Stockton and Darlington Railway. In some respects they were unsuited to sustained running, on account of having a small firebox for such a large boiler. Yet they worked surprisingly well on the S&DR where shipping mineral traffic on short runs involved much stopping and waiting, allowing the locomotives to build up steam at intervals. One such locomotive, the North Eastern Railway '1001' Class No. 1275 still exists today and is part of the collection at the National Railway Museum in York.

Bouch conducted additional activities over and above his

responsibilities for the S&DR, including acting as the engineer for the Weardale and Shildon Water Company which we shall return to soon.

Engineering was a vocation that William Bouch shared with another in his family. His brother, Sir Thomas Bouch, also set out on a career in railway engineering, starting as an assistant to one of the engineers constructing the Lancaster and Carlisle Railway. Like William, he later became a civil engineer for the S&DR, before moving on to a post as manager and engineer for the Edinburgh and Northern Railway.

Thomas's civil engineering feats included the design of many railway bridges and viaducts, though sadly he appears to now be best remembered for his design of the ill fated first Tay bridge in Scotland. A tragic incident cast a shadow on his otherwise worthy career when it collapsed under strong side winds in December 1879 as a train carrying passengers was crossing it.

William Bouch was not only a tutor and champion of the Institute and its facilities. He also served as a member of its committee, and for a time in the 1850s acted as its Treasurer. He also donated reading material for the benefit of the members.

He remained in charge of the Shildon Works until his death following several months of illness in 1876, the year after the fiftieth anniversary of the opening of the Stockton & Darlington Railway. His name lives on in Shildon as a consequence of having had a street above the Institute named after him. An obituary in the Northern Echo on 20 January 1876 included the following tribute:

"Among the community in which he dwelt, the late Mr Bouch will be greatly missed. Although failing health has of late prevented him from taking that interest in philanthropic objects which was his wont, yet he will long be remembered as one who laboured for the social improvement and intellectual elevation of those to whom opportunities were denied. He did his utmost to promote the interests of the Shildon Mechanics Institute, and was an earnest supporter of the Shildon Horticultural and Industrial Society, whose annual exhibitions have been unique in respect of the industrial competitions which they originated. In politics he was a steadfast and consistent Liberal. Taking him all in all, Mr Bouch will live in the recollection of all as one whose amiability endeared him to those who were intimate with him, and those whose abilities and sterling business qualities made him an important and respected member of the commercial community."

Bringing news to the people

In these modern times, where most of us carry a means to access news stories from around the world in the palms of their hands, it can be difficult to appreciate how challenging access to regional, national and world news once was.

A daily newspaper was an expensive luxury few working men and women could justify paying for, and acquiring one in 1833 wasn't easy. There was no such thing as a newsagent's shop in the Shildons. Newspapers at that time were dispatched directly to customers via the postal service, delivered to homes just as any other item of mail might be. The famous British Penny Post had not yet been introduced and, over and above the regular cost of postage for each newspaper, a tax of four pence had to be paid. That tax was reduced to one penny in 1836, three years after the founding of the Institute, but the tax was not abolished until 1855.

In order to bring regular news to its members, the Institute decided that taking out subscriptions to a number of newspapers should be a priority. This certainly seems to have become one of the contributory factors for more people joining and attending the Institute, as evidenced by an entry in the half-yearly report book in the summer of 1844 after a period in which they had suspended the service. It stated that during the previous six months attendance at the reading room had been unsatisfactory which the committee attributed to having stopped the delivery of newspapers by post. They subsequently re-subscribed to the newspapers to rectify the situation.

The following are some of the publications that the Institute made available during the 1840s. Many of these titles, like the Institute itself, were founded at the beginning of the 1830s:

Illustrated London News - a weekly publication that first appeared in May 1842 to become the world's first illustrated news magazine. With pictures spread generously throughout, this would have been quite novel and particularly interesting to members whose reading skills may not have been as strong as others. This publication continued to be printed until 2003.

Leeds Mercury - a venerable newspaper that had first been published in 1718. When the Institute subscribed to this, it was in the ownership of editor and publisher

Edward Baines who produced it weekly from his office in Briggate, Leeds. Later it was made available three times a week. It was available to purchase for sixpence and ceased publication in 1939.

Newcastle Journal - another local newspaper that has survived right through to the present day. The Journal was introduced in 1832. This was slightly more expensive than the Leeds Mercury, being seven pence to buy. Published from 69 Pilgrim Street in the city of Newcastle itself, the paper was available to readers across Northumberland, County Durham, Cumberland, Westmoreland, Yorkshire and the Scottish Borders. They also had agents in Dublin.

Durham Chronicle - a newspaper introduced in 1824 and published with the sub-title "or General Northern Advertiser". It described itself as a "political, literary, commercial and agricultural journal" and boasted that it was the most extensively circulated paper published between York and Newcastle. It was seven pence to buy, initially four pages long, printed at the company's office in Fleshgate, Durham, and made available every Saturday.

Tait's Magazine - an Edinburgh published magazine promoting liberal political views and news of contemporary cultural and literary matters. It regularly included essays by Thomas De Quincey who contrary to the political stance of the magazine was a Tory. In one issue his essay "A Tory's Account of Toryism, Whiggism and Radicalism" was punctuated by sarcastic replies thought to have been from the founder, William Tait.

The Penny Magazine - which was an illustrated weekly magazine aimed at the working classes and launched in 1832. Its owner was Charles Knight who had priced it at a penny per issue to deliberately make it affordable to the working classes. He kept the production price down by using woodcut printing rather than the higher quality steel engraved images. Again this paper presented a Whiggish political and radical religious worldview.

The Glasgow Mechanics Magazine - provided to the Institute through the generosity of Mr Oswald Gilkes, brother of Edward and a locomotive engineer himself. As the title reveals this was published in Trongate, Glasgow, by W R McPhun. It was first made available during the 1820s. Its contributors were civil engineers and practical mechanics, but articles often strayed into other scientific topics. Each issue cost three pence.

The Saturday Magazine - generously provided to the Institute by Edgar Gilkes, the iron founder and sometime evening tutor at the Institute. This was a British magazine published from 1832 to 1844 by the Committee of General Literature and Education, and an Anglican rival to the Penny Magazine. Each 4-page weekly issue was sold for 1 penny, or a subscriber could pay sixpence for monthly parts. Typically each issue began with an account of an exotic place somewhere in the world. The influence of the British Empire was expanding and people in England were very interested in the wider world. The magazine also covered items on nature, science, history and technology.

Chambers Journal - provided for the benefit of members by William Bouch. It was a sixteen page weekly magazine produced by William Chambers of Edinburgh. Again it was priced for the working class market, costing a penny per issue. It continued to be published until 1956.

The St James Chronicle - sent to the reading room by the Reverend James Manisty who was curate of St John's Church in Old Shildon. This paper started in 1761, cost sixpence per issue and was published three times per week. As you might expect, given the identity of the donor, the newspaper had a conformist Christian emphasis. It was published from London.

As you can see none of these were published daily, and evidence is documented that there were frequent debates as to whether a daily newspaper should be introduced to the reading room. In March 1848 a request was put out that all members desirous of having a daily newspaper sign their names to say that they would be prepared to pay sixpence per quarter to help cover the cost. Having gained the financial guarantee of the members a vote was held on which newspaper to purchase, and The Daily News was duly selected. Before long though, those members contributing the sixpence each quarter felt it unfair that they bore the burden for purchasing the papers. Consequently a number of measures were taken by the committee to reduce the cost.

Firstly, the Institute asked for day-old newspapers to be provided. This meant that the news was older, but the papers were cheaper and still being delivered daily. Secondly the Institute proposed to sell by tender all issues that had been in the reading room over two days from acquisition; in effect selling them on second-hand. There proved to be no willing buyers on this basis, so a new proposal was made which was that the papers could be paid for to be read on an evening elsewhere. This suggested arrangement attracted the attention of Mrs Dixon, landlady of The Locomotive Inn. A deal was struck for a charge of two shillings and sixpence.

In time other newspapers and periodicals were added to the subscribed newspaper list. Sometimes these replaced ones that had ceased to be printed, or had fallen out of favour with the members. By the mid 1850s readers could enjoy The Times, The Stockton & Darlington Times, The Bishop Auckland Herald, The Illustrated Times and the Yorkshire Herald.

Those readers seeking humour, satire or something lighter could revel in the pages of Punch, which launched in 1841, and later Judy or another publication simply entitled Fun.

New periodicals were added in the form of The Engineer, Blackwoods Magazine, Household Words and Leisure Hour. By the 1860s you could also peruse the pages of The Field, Cornhill Magazine, Once a Week, All the Year Round, Our Mutual Friend and Alliance. More newspapers were also added, such as The Star and Dial, the Manchester Examiner and Times and the Northern Daily Express. When the Northern Echo was launched it was added to the list of subscribed newspapers.

The number and range of periodicals waxed and waned according to both the tastes and interests of the times and the means of the Institute to procure them. In leaner times the number of subscribed publications was cut back to manageable and sustainable numbers.

This availability of newspapers and magazines was a gift to a community hungry for news. But not all visitors to the Institute were able to read them. The Institute made additional provision from time to time. For example, during the Crimean War, we are told, one of the members was tasked with reading aloud the news of the war to other members, from the only daily newspaper being delivered to the Institute, so that they might understand how the war was progressing.

By 1871 the Institute had taken to subscribing to the Musical Times which was supplied for the members enjoyment gratuitously by its editor. This was a period where community brass bands were booming, and there was much interest in choirs and musical performances. Several members of the New Shildon Saxhorn Band were members of the Institute, including its bandmaster Francis Dinsdale, and two promising young musical talents, Tom Bulch and George Allan, who would go on to compose enduring and famous band music. The Saxhorn Band would perform at Institute functions.

Another publication that tells us something about the membership of the Institute towards the latter part of the nineteenth century is The Women's Suffrage Journal. This offered news of events affecting all areas of women's lives, focusing particularly on features showing the breadth of support for women's suffrage across the United Kingdom. We know from the membership record books that there were several subscribing female members, and doubtless some of these were either interested in, or promoters of the Women's Suffrage movement.

As the availability of leisure time and geographic mobility across the region improved, we progress toward the 1890s and find that changes in organised sports brought a heightened interest in sporting matters. New periodicals met that need, such as the Sporting and Dramatic Times or Athletic News. The Bazaar Exchange and Mart gave people the opportunity to browse for a bargain. Other publications like Great Thoughts or perhaps Answers stimulated the mind, and occasionally more niche publications such as Vegetarian News were purchased.

The Books of William Denton

The Institute played a significant part in elevating some quite extraordinary characters throughout its history. One early member of the Institute followed a peculiar path of achievement that was quite different to that of many of his railway engineering colleagues. He would become almost unique in that some of his own literary work would eventually come to rest on the Institute's library shelves. For this to happen, though, he first had to go on a long journey.

William Denton was born on 8 January 1823, and subsequently christened on 9 February that year at St Cuthbert's Church in Darlington. It's worthy of note that as well as being a surname, Denton is the name of a hamlet a few miles west of Darlington from where his ancestral family may have originated.

William was the son of Robert Denton and his wife Jane. Writing in the 1870 part biography "William Denton, the Geologist and Radical, a biographical sketch", William's part-biographer J H Powell explains that the Denton family, like many at that time, were poor and lived in a single room. Powell documents how Robert Denton was a sturdy, true man, but also ignorant and uneducated. His wife Jane however, had attended a school and endeavoured to pass on some of her education. She also arranged for William to receive some rudimentary education from the age three, thanks to the aid of a kindly friend Nellie Sedgwick who maintained herself by keeping a small school.

The 1851 UK census shows a widowed Eleanor Sedgwick, listed as a Domestic Schoolmistress living with her daughter Ann on Darlington's Priestgate. This may have been 'Nelly Sedgwick', and if so she had been born in Sedgefield in around 1784 and would have been around 25 years old when teaching William, which clashes with Powell's description of Nellie being an 'old woman'. Teaching appears to have been a vocation passed down through the Sedgwick family women as, by 1861, Eleanor had passed away and her unmarried daughter Ann Sedgwick was also practicing as a teacher.

Jane Denton and Nellie Sedgwick set young William on a journey of learning and discovery that many of his peers did not emulate. His next place of learning was the British Penny School, though his education was further augmented by visits to the Methodist Library and regular attendance at Sunday School. He became inspired by the teacher William Shotton, a Baptist, who introduced him to practical subjects like Phrenology and Electricity. Shotton demonstrated experiments in the latter subject with a galvanic battery of his own. Roughly around this same time, Denton received an introduction to Geology and acquired a geologists hammer of his own. This was to become his great passion.

At age ten, William signed the Temperance Pledge and at eleven he worked for a currier, in the leather processing industry. He was earning a half-crown a week. In religious terms William and his father discovered a new path of progressive Methodism, a less classical approach to this religious format which allowed for more theological exploration and intellectual freedom. This path placed young William at odds with older men he worked with at the leather works, so his next move was to find employment at a grocery store.

At the same time he graduated to grammar-school where study of the classical languages entered his curriculum.

Robert Denton's work made him ill, and in times of illness William noted how the family received none of the charity professed by the Methodists. When Robert eventually recovered he took up new work as a 'hawker' carrying a basket of wares to sell on the streets. He did well at this; so well in fact that he was eventually in a position to run a shop, not in Darlington, but in that steadily growing community of New Shildon.

With the family now relocated to the rail engineering town, in around 1837, at age fourteen, the bright young lad William was apprenticed to Timothy Hackworth, to learn the trade of machinist. William's education by this time would have made him a useful asset to Hackworth's workforce. Powell's biography describes that William worked on iron by day and explored geology at night. His work and wage enabled him access to the books and resources of New Shildon Mechanics Institute.

The excavation of the Prince of Wales Tunnel under Shildon was a major opportunity for William. He hunted for geological specimens amongst the debris from the tunnel workings, occasionally finding what he understood to be fossils.

He gave lectures on Temperance and addresses on Religion at the Methodist Sunday School. He also became part of a group of around half-a dozen young men that would engage in debate at any opportunity. His quest for new views and opinions on the world brought him George Combe's controversial book "Constitution of Man." This interest was met with scorn by William's Minister who denounced it as dangerous. Later a visit to the Shildons by the preacher Joseph Barker also introduced a Barkerite influence to William's thinking, resulting in his removing buttons from his coat.

It was a dispute over principles and values that caused a nineteen year old William to leave the employment of Timothy Hackworth. The pioneering engineer had requested that Denton go to a brewery to fulfil a job to repair some machinery there. This errand offended the young Temperance advocate who was vocal in his protestation.

"Conscience!" Hackworth raged, infuriated by the stubbornness of his apprentice. "You have got your conscience as fine as a needle point. You shall go." To this Denton expressed that he could not consent. "Then you can go home," said Hackworth.

William did continue at the Soho Works for a short time after this, but the division between master and apprentice proved irreconcilable and the young man was thrown out of his apprenticeship before completing it. He now needed new work, and applied to the Normal Institute, a teacher training college at

Borough Road in London. He was admitted as a student and later appointed to teach in Newport, Monmouthshire.

The Temperance movement was not strong in Newport and many Ministers there also drank. Denton took to preaching as well as teaching, and received stern treatment from publicans such that he made a 'legion of foes.' He also took to writing in this period and moved to Ashford, Kent from where ie issued his first essay on the deleterious effects of tobacco. There he also found foes and his radical lectures were opposed by the orthodoxy, which resulted in his being manhandled on occasion.

Above: William Denton, born in Darlington and apprenticed to Timothy Hackworth, he became a world renowned geologist and religious radical whose books were sent from America to be added to the Institute's library collection

He decided to emigrate to make a new start in America, arriving in Philadelphia in 1848. Soon after, the five or six sovereigns that he had taken with him to start his new life were stolen, so he decided to look up an old friend who had moved further inland to Pottsville, a hundred miles away. He hitched a ride on the rear car of a coal train, charming the brakeman into allowing him to remain on the journey. The trip proved fruitless, and William had to return to Philadelphia, a journey he reportedly attempted by the same means accompanied by a Mexican soldier he had met.

Now penniless, he pawned his pocket watch to secure a small sum of money and again found some work teaching, before applying at a machine shop to work as a clerk. His fortunes improved such that he sent for his family, and his sweetheart Caroline Gilbert, whom he had met in Ashford. The couple were married soon after Caroline's arrival in Philadelphia, but their joy was short lived. Caroline died and this affected William profoundly. He left Philadelphia and travelled to Guyandotte, in West Virginia, where he settled in solitude before again sending for his family.

William's next move was to Dayton to accept another teaching post before moving to a better one in Cincinnati, which is where he met American born Elizabeth Melissa Foote, originally from Williamstown and around three years his junior, who was working as a type compositor. Elizabeth, no adherent of conventional fashion, had taken a liking to the 'bloomer costume', and William had his work set out shielding her from resultant insult. On 15 August 1854 the couple married in Geauga, Ohio.

In 1860 the couple were living at the village of Painesville in Lake County Ohio where their first son Sherman Foote Denton was born in 1857 and first daughter Shelley Wright Denton was born in 1860. Their other children were; William Dixon Denton in Feb 1865, Robert Winsford in March 1868 and finally Caroline 'Carrie' Delynia Denton in May 1869.

Denton saw the life of a writer and travelling lecturer as a route out of teaching, with which he had become frustrated, and produced a first book "Common Sense Thoughts on the Bible." Once the first edition was published, William and Elizabeth bought printing equipment and used their combined skills to produce a second run of 5,000 books. He followed this with "Poems for Reformers." He also campaigned against slavery. His lecturing tours took him through the northern states and into Canada. He became joint editor of a weekly publication "The Social Revolution" before a move to Kansas where he bought 160 acres of land, on which he planted 3,000 fruit trees before making yet another move to Cleveland just before the outbreak of the American Civil War.

The war gave him opportunity for a quieter life during which he turned his attention back to Geology. With wife Elizabeth he wrote "The Soul of Things," a treatise on psychometry, followed by "Our Planet, Its Past and Future." Remarkably at least one copy of this made its way to Britain, to be presented to be added to the library at the Institute.

In the Institute's half yearly report for the period ending 31 December 1870, Secretary William Robinson wrote

"There has also been presented to the Institute the book written by Mr Denton, formerly of this village and employed at Shildon Works many years ago (called Our Planet) kindly presented by Mr MacNay."

A copy of "The Soul of Things; or Psychometric Research and Discoveries" also found its way to the Institute. Secretary, P H Greenwell's half-yearly report for the period ending 31 December 1871 read

"Only one book has been added, viz. "The Soul of Things" presented by the author William Denton of Boston America, who was formerly a member of this Institute."

William travelled quite extensively as a geological surveyor and lecturer, and returned to Britain briefly in 1877, taking time to visit the town of his birth. His last expedition was to Australia, new Zealand and New Guinea. He died on the 26 August 1883, the date on which the volcano at Krakatoa, between South Sumatra and Java, exploded violently. Some British newspapers of the day reported that William was killed in this explosion. The Carnarvon and Denbigh Herald of Friday 30 November 1883 is one example.

"A cable despatch announces the death of Professor Denton, who is well-known as a geologist and lecturer. He has been travelling for the last two years accompanied by his two sons, Shelby and Sherman, engaged in lecturing and in scientific exploration in Australia, new Zealand and China. He was supposed to have been in Java at the time of his death, and, it is probable, was a victim of the earthquake in that country. Nothing has been received except the cable message announcing his death, and that the sons would start immediately for home. Professor Denton was born on January 8th, at Darlington. He has visited nearly every portion of the civilised world, and as a geologist had won a high reputation."

The truth behind the circumstances of his death however is a little less dramatic. William's son, Sherman, wrote a book entitled "Incidents of a Collector's Rambles in Australia, New Zealand and

New Guinea". The book makes clear that William Denton died of fever in the jungle interior of New Guinea, bringing the expedition to a premature end. New Zealand newspapers such as the 13 October 1883 issue of the Auckland Star confirm this to be true:

"Captain Armit (special correspondent of the Melbourne "Argus") and the members of his expedition arrived here from New Guinea. Only one of the party is free from fever. Captain Armit reports that Professor Denton, the American geologist, who was accompanying him to New Guinea, died from exhaustion after a severe attack of fever on the 26th August. (Professor Denton will be remembered as having delivered a series of lectures in Auckland)"

Captain Armit had been the first of the expedition to contract a fever, but had pulled through as William Denton was succumbing to it. He noted in a later account of the incident that Denton had believed that he could overcome the illness without taking any of the medicines that the expedition carried, which was possibly an extension of his Temperance beliefs. The expedition party had been attempting to return with Denton when, weakened by the disease, he passed away during the night in the their shared tent. His colleagues buried him between two mountains before completing their return.

The expedition, in search of valuable resources and minerals with a view to expanding the British Empire, had been backed by the Melbourne Argus newspaper, and was competing with a rival expedition launched by the Age newspaper.

Selected books published by William Denton:

- Poems For Reformers (1856)
- Our Planet - Its Past and Future or Lectures on Geology (1869)
- The Soul of Things (1870)
- The Irreconcilable Records, or Genesis and Geology (1870)
- Radical Discourse on Religious Subjects (1872)
- The Deluge in the Light of Modern Science (1872)
- Radical Rhymes (1873)
- Be Thyself (1880)
- The Grace of Ministry Considered as a Divine Gift of Uninterrupted Transmission and Two-Fold Character (1880)

- Common Sense Thoughts on the Bible for Common Sense People
- Is Darwin Right, or The Origin of Man (1881)

Above: A contemporary depiction from 1883 of the death of William Denton (centre) from who succumbed to fever while exploring the interior of New Guinea. The Institute today holds several of his books.

A Quest for Water

The committee of the institute were not solely concerned with the provision of education and recreation for the people of New Shildon. It was apparent to members and committee that there was much about the still relatively young town that was far from satisfactory, and the Institute threw itself into campaigns for improvements for the welfare of its members and community.

One essential resource required by both the people of New Shildon and the railway company for which the majority of them worked, was a supply of water. There were, and still are though they are difficult to notice, three streams that converge in the area. These ran shallow and could not be relied upon in summer.

To address their own needs the Stockton & Darlington Railway created a large cistern to collect water which was pumped to it from a stream. This however was for washing locomotives and supplying boilers. The public were prevented from being able to access it.

There were also three private wells that had been sunk. The water from these was sold to the public by their owners. The price per bucket made this prohibitive to many families. As a consequence, you can imagine that health and personal hygiene were not as could be desired.

In 1845, the Institute resolved to find a solution to obtaining an increased water supply to the village. A sub-committee was formed comprising of William MacNay, a managing engineer at the Shildon Works, E B Humble and J B Thorpe. They set about investigating the possibilities. In 1847 a report was presented back by the young engineer Daniel Adamson, son of the owner of the coaching inn at Old Shildon.

The report communicated the frustrated state of the venture, explaining that a team had attempted to dig a well in a field belonging to the Pease family to secure a water supply, and having dug down 23 feet no water was reached. The well had then become too narrow to accommodate a workman. Further depth was reached using boring equipment to a depth of 25 feet whereupon it struck a layer of blue slate and ironstone. On this discovery they abandoned the venture.

The next exploration was upon land near a Mrs Applegarth's house where there was a spring. The flow of the spring was measured and found to produce 1,190 gallons of water per day. Plans were drawn-up to lay pipes to bring this water across the fields to a point near the residential area of New Shildon. The cost assessment of the planned operation proved it to be too expensive for the Institute and they was compelled to withdraw from the scheme, lamenting the great benefit that would have been derived had they been in a position to proceed.

This objective of obtaining a reliable source of water wasn't intended to be purely for the benefit of the Institute. The committee had a wider beneficial objective in mind, as we can see from this report in the Durham Chronicle of Friday 24 September 1847:

"The Committee of that spirited little society, the

Shildon Mechanics Institute, have it in agitation to build baths and wash-houses at the end of the village. The plan is a feasible one, and we hope they carry it out."

The noble objective, though deemed feasible, was harder to achieve than commentators might have hoped. The plans were yet to come to fruition by 7 January 1848 when the Newcastle Courant added a further tit-bit of news:

"The Committee of the New Shildon Mechanics Institute are carrying out sanitary measures in that district. Water being scarce, they have spent an amount of labour and some money in trying to get a better supply, although, as yet, their efforts have not been crowned with success."

In his Centenary account of the Institute Francis Bainbridge theorises that as New Shildon was founded on land that overlapped four separate townships, the four respective authorities that held influence over these had neglected the new town, largely on account of the fact that each had little influence or spending power anyway. What changed the situation was the increasing demand for water for locomotives which compelled the wealthy railway company to do something. Being a company of significant means, they made swift progress.

An assessment of the options available suggested that the best approach would be a major undertaking to bring water to Shildon from the hills of Weardale. A survey was conducted, and a consequent bill was promoted in Parliament. The Weardale and Shildon Waterworks Company was incorporated in 1866. This passing of a Parliamentary bill was cause for great celebration in the community. The Teesdale Mercury reported how the bells of St John's church rang out at the arrival of the much anticipated news and many locomotives and buildings were draped with flags proclaiming wishes of success to the new water company. There was a celebratory procession of men through the town, headed by the New Shildon Saxhorn Band, and guns and fog signals were reported to have been fired through the day.

The passing of this Act of Parliament also meant that the Institute was relieved of its role in spearheading the mission to secure a water supply. It did, however, play a significant role in bringing pressure to bear and acting as champions.

Promoting Green-Fingered Pastimes

Another major campaign undertaken by the Institute for the benefit of the village, was to attempt to secure land upon which the people of New Shildon might grow their own vegetables and pursue horticulture as a hobby. At the Institute's half-yearly meeting at the end of 1846, the committee noted in their report a strong recommendation that a system of garden allotment should be carried out.

As with the water supply, however, it was not easy to secure the means. A short article in the Newcastle Courant of 21 April 1848 tells of the committee's frustrations around that time, particularly given that some others were succeeding in the same goal:

> "J. Smithson Esq., has set apart two fields at Chapel-row, Shildon, for the purpose of spade husbandry, and has let them to the miners. They are working very industriously at their little plots when not employed in the pits. The New Shildon Mechanics Institute endeavoured to get land for the inhabitants of their village, but though not fortunate enough to secure it this season, they expect to do so next."

Bainbridge's book marking the Institute's Centenary explains that various plots of ground were indeed eventually leased as allotment land, and the spoil bank that had been created through the excavation of the Prince of Wales Tunnel was also given over to the railwaymen for cultivation. The new hobby flourished. The town appears to have held its first Horticultural and Industrial Society exhibition at the end of August 1869.

The Institute continued to provide allotment land until well into the twentieth century, and when its most recent building was created on Redworth Road a significant allocation of land behind that building was originally given over to allotments. Some of this was later converted to become a car park and the rest sold as building land to accommodate both the newer portion of Adamson Street and part of Harrison Close.

Receiving A Good Talking To

Another benefit that senior influential figures connected to the Institute wanted to bring to members was the opportunity to hear talks from experts on particular subjects that they, or indeed the wider public, would not otherwise get to hear. As a result the committee placed significant effort over the early decades of in securing guest speakers to deliver lectures.

You might assume, with the Institute being focused initially on scientific and technical knowledge, that all of the lectures would have fallen into this category, yet this was not so. Whether finding affordable speakers on technical subjects was perhaps more difficult or expensive than anticipated, or perhaps through the committee being agreeable to catering for broader interests, the range of subjects covered at these talks was surprisingly diverse.

There was a definite pronounced emphasis on social and moral improvement, with those engaging the speakers often choosing subjects that were designed to improve the behaviour and life choices of the listener.

Sometimes the orators were from far afield, perhaps brought to New Shildon expressly for each engagement, or else opportunistically booked whilst touring the country with a talk on a particular subject. At other times the lecturer was more local, and sometimes a member of the Institute. Occasionally it might be someone renowned in their field that might be persuaded to speak by the more influential officers of the organisation.

The talks increasingly included an accompanying visual entertainment or demonstration. This might take the form of practical experiments, or increasingly the use of illustrations courtesy of the invention of the Magic Lantern, a predecessor of the slide projector. The magic lantern wasn't a particularly new idea. It had technological origins in the mid Seventeenth Century, with portable models increasingly available in the decades after the Institute was founded. These and were sometimes used by travelling 'Professors', essentially showmen, who even occasionally used sound effects to bring their illuminated shows to life for their audiences.

The committee often wrote, within their half-yearly reports, about the success of, or otherwise disappointing attendance at, the lectures they had organised. In addition to lectures, the Institute also hosted sessions called 'penny readings' where members of the community with poor reading skills might attend the reading room, for a fee of one penny. Here they listened to a well practiced and entertaining reader relate select articles of news from the newspapers and periodicals. Occasionally these sessions also incorporated a musical entertainment, usually from New Shildon's resident Saxhorn Band.

The following list of some of the lecture subjects delivered in the Institute's early years, selected from documented evidence, gives you a sense of the range of interests and topics covered.

Year	Subject	Speaker
1847	Popular Astronomy	John Pickering
1848	Teesdale and the Lead Mines	F P Cockshott
1850	The Human Frame	Rev. J B Dawson
1851	The Rise of Railways	Joseph Pease
1853	Poetry	Rev. T McCullagh
1859	Self Help	William Bouch
1859	Manliness	Richard Pickering
1859	Social Economy	John Pickering
1859	Shakespeare - The Poet	Christopher Johnson
1859	Edmund Burke - Parliamentarian	C Simpson
1859	Life & Writing of Oliver Goldsmith	Mr Gatenby
1859	Difference of Opinion	Mr Douthwaite
1859	Pneumatics with Experiments	Samuel Hannah
1859	Scraps of Knowledge	John Peart
1859	Mirror of Nature	Christopher Johnson
1859	England's Progress	James Oliver
1859	Poem on the Village	John Richmond
1859	Uses of Great Men	Christopher Johnson
1860	Overland Route to India	D MacNay
1860	Progress of the Railways	John Glass
1860	Selection from Pickwick Papers	G H Robinson
1860	Xmas After a Long Absence	J Danson
1861	Dickens Shooting Party	G E Alexander
1861	Irish Dialogue	C Hogwood
1861	Hogarth's Pictures	J C Oliver
1861	Captain Cook	C Simpson
1861	Working Men	J Storey
1861	Power of Example	R Pickering
1861	Co-operation	R Jaques
1861	Turkish Baths	Dr Lang
1861	Abraham Lincoln	William Bouch
1861	Questions From Shakespeare	G Bowman
1861	Tom Hood	J Dixon
1861	Phrenology (3 lectures)	Mr Butterworth
1862	The Reason Why	Mr Manson

1862	Pneumatics	J Hannah
1862	Mechanical Effects of Steam	John J Platts
1862	Study of Words	Rev. Thomas Davies
1862	Chemistry of Bread	Rev. T F Hardwicke
1862	Animal Physiology	Mr Manson
1862	The Exodus of the Israelites	Rev. W M Hitchcock
1867	Compulsory Education	John J Platts
1867	Abolition of Capital Punishment	G Spence
1868	Abstinence	R Armstrong
1868	Phrenology	Mr Burns
1869	A Man's a Man For Aa' That	Rev. H Phillips
1869	Impressions of London	Rev. J J Hillocks
1870	Borneo	Mr Baines
1870	Scientific Lecture	Mr Wheeler
1871	Invention of the Locomotive	John W Hackworth
1873	Sanitary Science & the Water Cure	Dr Munro
1875	Learning	Mr Parry
1877	Grand Centennial Exhibition	Theodore West
1885	Milan, Genoa, Naples, Venice	Henry Fell Pease JP
1887	Acoustic & Electrical Discoveries	E Cox Walker MSTE
1887	Icebergs & Glaciers in SW Durham	Dr Manson
1887	Colours & Colour Blindness	Dr Radcliffe Gaylord
1894	Health & Home	Miss Lottie Dunn
1895	Sound	Mr R J Patterson
1895	Air and Water	Mr Joseph Stoker
1895	Historical Art	Mr J B Bowman

There are slight shifts in the subject matter from the moral and spiritual to more literary, scientific and technological matters as the years go by, perhaps due to the advances in science made across those decades giving speakers new things to talk about. It is interesting to see, also, how talks were given on other parts of the world, presumably based on experiences in an age when few could afford long distance travel.

Grand Days Out at Affordable Prices

Another benefit the Institute brought to New Shildon was the opportunity to partake in organised affordable excursions, usually to the coast or some other natural beauty spot. These were special days when groups of friends or even whole families could travel together. They would involve a large cross-section of the community coming together to enjoy the experience at the same time. The Institute would make arrangements to commission an entire train through its association with the Stockton & Darlington Railway Company. They would then sell tickets at a discounted rate. The trips were usually arranged for a date in the summer months, when the weather would be at its best.

The excursions were priced with an intention to make a small profit to help the Institute with its running costs, and to first and foremost provide the service to members, thereby encouraging membership. The committee also believed that hosting and organising the trips would create a connection between the Institute and the rest of the townspeople, with the latter regarding the Institute more kindly and perhaps consequently considering making more use of its educational facilities. This was Victorian relationship building and networking at work.

One of the earliest excursions recorded took place on 29 June 1844, whereupon two hundred and fifty people boarded a train at Shildon to travel to Middlesborough. From there they then boarded a ship that took them by sea to Whitby. Sadly the excursion had not been entirely satisfactory to either organisers or passengers. To begin with the railway company had provided open wagons for the rail journey, exposing travellers to the elements. Then at Middlesborough the organisers learned that the ship they had chartered, the "British Queen," had been substituted by its owner who replaced it with a larger vessel. This replacement ship had not taken sufficient ballast on board, resulting in it being quite unsteady in the water which created an unpleasant motion throughout the voyage.

The annual excursion the following year, 1845, was expected to be a repeat of the previous year's day out, but ended up being afflicted in a more serious way. It was a Monday morning when the special train set off from Shildon, and during the journey, around a quarter of a mile from Stockton station, it encountered a coal train heading in the opposite direction on the same line.

The driver of the coal train saw the special train heading his way and opened up his locomotive thinking that he might be able to get his train onto the Middlesborough branch line before the tourist train reached him. He had hoped this might provide a solution to avert disaster. Unfortunately for him some of his coal wagons left the rails and became stuck upon the route in the way of the oncoming excursion train. The result was a dreadful collision. The tender of the oncoming train was dragged up over the locomotive and many passengers behind were injured. One passenger, Mr Oliver, received a serious back injury and it was felt that he might never recover.

In their report at the end of December that year the committee noted that:

"The whole of the parties who were unfortunately injured were visited by a deputation of the committee, and relief was extended both in a pecuniary manner and otherwise where it seemed to be required. Amongst these was one case which was marked by particular destitution, which your committee thought it desirable to procure a mattress, pay for medical attention, and engage a nurse to provide refreshing articles as the doctor recommended."

Though these the events could hardly have been attributed to any negligence on the part of the Institute it would be easy to see how in current safety-conscious times such an incident may have resulted in the abandonment of any future plans to hold excursions. Fortunately, the Institute were not deterred, and made careful efforts in arranging further trips in the years that followed so that both members and community were able to enjoy them without further incident.

1847 saw a pleasure trip to Frosterley in Weardale, which had a smaller attendance than previous trips, and consequently only made a penny in profit. By 1848 it was possible to get all the way to the newly thriving resort town of Redcar by rail, so the Institute made that its destination of choice and continued to do so for many tears after. On that first Redcar trip, the committee had a few admonishing words about the train provided by the S&DR:

"A very great number of people availed themselves of the privilege, and everything passed off in a comfortable and pleasant manner, with but one or two exceptions. We would direct your attention to the subject of being obliged to put up with trucks unseated and unswept, and think that Mr Geo. Stephenson ought to be spoken to, and in future the trucks done away with — they are neither comfortable nor convenient. We also think that there ought to be some reduction in the price of the trucks."

By the time of the 1850 trip to Redcar the number of passengers enjoying the day out had swollen to 2,200 and the Institute realised a profit of fifty pounds, seventeen shillings and ten pence.

Other destinations were occasionally chosen. In 1857 a

'cheap night excursion' was arranged taking people to Manchester, via a connection at Preston Junction, to visit the grand Art Treasures Exhibition held there. Other years saw the Institute venture elsewhere, including to Stanhope Castle, where a picnic was organised in 1870, or further afield to Hull as in 1861. Generally however, it was the trips to towns on the north-east coast such as Redcar, Saltburn Whitby and Scarborough which attracted the most participation.

Time for Tea

Even in the early days, before the organisation had its own hall in which to host celebrations, the community of New Shildon would usually look to the Institute to organise, and be at the heart of, any celebration of note. As any important milestone or notable event approached, a sub-committee would be appointed to organise and make arrangements. Unlike our grand celebrations today, where one might expect to see wine or champagne flowing freely, the central feature in those days was tea.

Tea is something we take very much for granted today. It is our go-to drink at any time of the day. Yet the 'tea party', with all formality of a dressed table and appropriate tablewares, was very much a Victorian fashion. Prior to the period we're exploring here, the tea that we drank in England was usually imported from China. The 1830s brought change, through the creation of the first tea estates in India, which became very much a part of the British colonial import and export network. By the beginning of the Victorian era, tea had become accessible to most households, even those of the working classes. Though the 'tea party' had become an increasingly common event for the wealthier classes, such events, and all the ceremony that came with them, was something reserved for very special occasions among workers.

It's worthy of further note that although such celebrations were announced as being "tea" parties, substantial quantities of coffee were also served.

One of the first tasks for any such celebration would be to identify a suitable venue, one large enough to host the party. At the time of those very first Institute tea parties there were no suitable purpose built halls in New Shildon. The nearest best thing was to temporarily requisition another suitably large space. For example, a party held one Thursday evening in December 1848 used a new joiner's workshop building that had recently been erected on the works site, and that had been swept, cleaned up and furnished for the occasion.

The committee reported, after the event, that the sub-committee for that particular event had been split into seven groups, each expected to focus on arranging a different aspect of the party. We've already mentioned that one of these groups arranged the venue, but what of the other groups?

As the list of invitees was not limited to the ladies and gentlemen of New Shildon, one group took responsibility for making sure that guests from further afield had accommodation for the evening, and also for arranging the attendance of speakers to address the event. Another sub-group took responsibility for decorating venue, often using evergreen boughs and foliage from the Brusselton and Redworth woods. Walls were decorated with paintings, antlers, stuffed animals and birds, coats of arms of the local gentry, banners of local societies and working drawings of machinery. A third group took responsibility for ensuring seating, tables and platforms. A fourth group set about ensuring the purchase of spiced, and plain, bread for the tables, along with teacakes. A fifth group engaged the band to provide the musical entertainment, as well as ensuring plentiful supply of milk, sugar, tea and coffee. The final group made provision for hot water and sourced ladies and waiters to make and distribute the drinks.

Quite often there would be a visual centrepiece on display at the event; something specially created for the day that would draw attention and create conversation. At the 1848 annual tea party that was a 'diorama', a three dimensional miniature model, that had been built by one of the workmen at the railway works. There were other main features that year, such as a huge side aspect drawing of the locomotive "Rokeby," and working model steam engines.

These tea parties were generally reported to have been hugely successful and quite often over-subscribed as more people turned out than could be accommodated. For that tea party we described as being held in 1848, which was of course presided over by Timothy Hackworth himself, we are told in the committee's report that six hundred and fifty places had been set, but that eight hundred and fifty people had attended. As you might imagine this created quite a crush. Outside the December evening was clear sharp and frosty, but inside the joiners shop the atmosphere was said to have been that of a fairy-land in summer.

At the conclusion of each event special trains would be waiting to return attendees that had travelled from Bishop Auckland or Darlington, towns close enough to not need to stay over.

These December tea parties were repeated each year. An account from the Darlington & Stockton Times of 28 December 1850 describes the decorative spectacle greeting attendees as they listened to the music produced by the Darlington Quadrille Band:

> We observed amongst other mural decorations, a stuffed fox (with a lemon inserted in his mouth) surrounded by green boughs; beneath Reynard was a medieval looking shield; on either hand a landscape painting; and above a representation in colours of a dead rabbit and some carrots. Near at hand was a plethoric cupid, leering wickedly at an orange suspended near him: upon the almost concealed platform at a little distance were two large vases of stone or plaster, - backed by two fine stags heads and a drawing ("life size") of a locomotive and fronted by a woodcock and some grouse; whilst above all were suspended, in cages, some feathered songsters, whose sylvan notes curiously mingled with the clatter of cups and saucers, and the busy hum of conversation.

What a spectacle. Can you imagine suspending songbirds in cages above an indoor banquet in modern times?

After the death of Timothy Hackworth in 1850, the tea parties were presided over by other senior supporters of the Institute. In 1851 Joseph Pease took the chair, and other members of the Pease family, Henry and Joseph Whitwell Pease, were present. Prominent places were reserved for other grandees and supporters such as Edgar Gilkes, once of Shildon but by then living at Middlesborough, and speakers, such as Edwin Paxton-Hood.

Speeches were always a central feature of the tea parties, and a select succession of senior figures would take the platform to address those present. The emphasis of the speeches was always broadly the same; pride in the achievements of the Stockton & Darlington Railway Company and the contribution New Shildon made toward those impressive outcomes. In his address to the Institute in 1850, Joseph Pease recalled his first visit to the area with George Stephenson to survey the valley. He spoke of being up to his knees in mire and water, and what a "boggy, swampy hole" it was. His companion that day had had to climb trees to get a view of the country surrounding them. Pease spoke of what had been achieved, and opined that if that survey had not been done then it would probably consequently not have been possible to travel by train to London or any other part of the country. The second key message related by speakers was the importance of the Institutes at Shildon and elsewhere, for the opportunities they presented to working people, giving them tools and knowledge to elevate themselves. This notion of taking responsibility for your own life goals was very much part of the Victorian psyche. Finally much was made of moral and social virtues of workmen and how they might be improved.

At the tea party held in 1858 it was the turn of Henry Pease, a Member of Parliament as well as official of the S&DR, to occupy the chair. By that point the committee had decided that to organise a tea party every year was too challenging an undertaking. They resolved that they would limit the events to intervals of three-or-four years. Henry Pease noted this suggestion and deemed it a sensible decision. In some ways the parties had become victims of their own success. Owing to their exceptional nature and quality, maintaining such expectations on an annual cycle had become unsustainable.

Another speaker at the tea party in 1858 was Daniel Adamson, son of the coach house owner in the town, who was a devotee of the Institute having been one of its earliest members while he had been apprenticed to Timothy Hackworth. Adamson was by then establishing a significant engineering reputation of his own through his work in manufacturing steam boilers in the Manchester area. His message to the people in attendance was that he attributed much of that success to his connection with the Institute.

In 1863 an important decision was made, which was to change the timing of the annual tea party such that, instead of taking place after Christmas, it would happen in September to align to the anniversary of the opening of the Stockton & Darlington Railway. This continued to be the practice for several years, but proved far from satisfactory. Organisers found that their New Shildon celebrations clashed with others organised in the railway company's principal towns of Darlington and Stockton. This in turn made it difficult for the key figures to attend the Shildon events. Eventually the tea parties were discontinued, except to mark particularly significant milestones such as the 50th anniversary of the S&DR, which we will arrive at in a future chapter.

Daniel Adamson

Daniel Adamson had been born on 30 April 1820. He was born into a large family with fifteen children. His father, also named Daniel, was a farmer and the proprietor of what became the Grey Horse public house on the outskirts of Old Shildon, which he ran with his wife Ann.

Young Daniel received his initial education courtesy of a Quaker school in Old Shildon, and did sufficiently well as to be apprenticed, aged thirteen, by Timothy Hackworth at his works. He also became one of the early members of the library and its later incarnation, the Institute. By the time of the 1841 census his father had passed away and his mother, Ann, was running the inn. Daniel continued to live there helping out whilst working for Hackworth.

In 1841 he completed his apprenticeship, and by 1850 he had risen from being a draughtsman and engineer, through being superintendent of stationary engines, to becoming a General Manager at the Soho Works.

Around the same time as Timothy Hackworth died, in 1850, Adamson found a new opportunity as a foundry manager in Stockport. The census year of 1851 saw Daniel living at 1 New Road, Heaton Norris with his wife Mary (née Pickard) and two daughters. He then set up a small iron works in Newton, Cheshire specialising in boiler and engine manufacture to meet the increasing demand for steam power. He took his inspiration from Hackworth's earlier designs but, possibly enabled by a keen and refined ability to research and learn, was quick to improve the designs and use pioneering new methods.

In 1872 he created his Daniel Adamson & Company factory at Dukinfield. He continued to press innovation throughout his manufacturing career, and lodged no fewer than nineteen patents whilst building a substantial reputation.

Adamson was unable to forget his home town and was invited back to speak at Institute events on several occasions, whereupon he would talk about how important an influence and opportunity membership had been in his own development. We saw earlier that he appeared as a speaker at the 1858 annual tea party. He was invited again in 1875 to speak at a special celebration to mark fifty years of the Stockton and Darlington Railway.

On that occasion he had to send his apologies on account of not being able to attend though a prior commitment, and instead provided the committee with a letter to be read out at the meeting. He did, though, make a special visit to New Shildon the following year, during which he offered a special audience in conjunction with the Institute at the British Schoolroom. This was attended by five-hundred-and-twenty guests. He was introduced to the room by the then President of the Institute, John Glass, who recalled Adamson as a school classmate. Glass told of how their schoolmaster,

Jonathan Dryden, had presented a particularly fiendish question to the class, and stated that none of the 'day scholars' could solve it. Glass had apparently replied "Oh, yes, there's Danny Adamson and one or two that could soon do it," as a measure of how even then Adamson had created the impression of being a bright young boy with much promise. Adamson then regaled the audience entertainingly with an outline of his life and career. He was afterwards presented with a "handsomely illuminated address" in tribute by William MacNay.

Above: Daniel Adamson, son of the former coach house keeper and former apprentice of Hackworth who went on to become a renowned engineer and industrialist.
From a portrait once held by the Institute.

Apart from his own factory, Adamson had a number of

additional business interests and investments including mill building, steel and iron works. He is best remembered perhaps for his advocacy for the Manchester Ship Canal project, championing it with a zeal that resulted in his being depicted in newspaper cartoons of the day. The initiative to drive this solution forward was successful and after the enabling Act of Parliament was passed, in 1885, he became the first Chairman of the Board of the Manchester Ship Canal Company.

He was a founder of the Iron and Steel Institute and a member of many other influential organisations of his day including the Institution of Civill Engineers, The British Iron Trades Association, the Railway and Canal Traders Association, the Geological Society of London and the Manchester Literary and Philosophical Society.

Sadly he did not live to see the completion of the canal. He passed away in Didsbury on 13 January 1890. His legacy is celebrated in a number of ways. There are blue plaques in Didsbury and Adamson Street in Dukinfield. Adamson Street in Shildon, adjacent to the current Institute building, is also named in his honour.

A Place of Our Own at Last

Up until the 1850s, the Institute had managed reasonably well conducting its activities without a dedicated building to call its own. The members had the leased reading room at the Masons Arms at their disposal, while committee meetings took place in the S&DR Works drawing office. Celebrations took place in requisitioned workshops at either of the two engineering works and any lectures were presented at the British School. But this, still relatively young, town was continuing to grow, and with it grew the membership of the Institute. By 1851 the committee had begun to sow seeds of a new idea, having predicted the organisation's needs for greater capacity. The committee's half-yearly report at the end of that year stated:

> Your committee would express the hope that with increased facilities for improvement, the moral, social and intellectual enjoyments of the members of the Institute, and the inhabitants of the village may be promoted.

A year and a half later this desire was coming under a stronger focus:

> The report your committee have to present showing as it does an increased circulation of books, and a very large addition to the stock, exhibits the Institute to be in a very prosperous state, and the time has arrived for enlarged operations, and your committee have pleasure in stating that arrangements have been made for an enlarged Reading Room with separate ones for Library, committee meetings, classes, and other purposes, available for lectures, and conversational gatherings of members.

Despite the positivity of this preceding report, the arrangements mentioned were not to be swiftly fulfilled. Two years later in the summer report for 1855 the matter was mentioned once again.

> That this meeting being deeply impressed with the necessity of having increased accommodation for the Library and Reading room, request their committee to take vigorous and energetic measures during the ensuing half-year, either for building a new room or materially enlarging the present one.

Some of the most influential members of the Institute, William Bouch, manager of the Works, Mr Robson, Mr MacNay, Mr Graham and Mr Snaith, were formed into a sub-committee to try to influence the financiers of the railway company, and to examine and assess prospective locations. Through the years that followed, members of the Institute were encouraged either to take a share in the New Shildon Building Society, or raise money by whatever other means they could toward the organisation's goal.

The Durham Chronicle of 29 January 1858 reports on the half yearly meeting at the end of 1857 in which a breakthrough was reported relating to the committee's progress in petitioning the railway company for a new building:

> The attention of the committee had been especially directed to the increased necessity for a new building for the use of its members, and had pleasure in stating that they had succeeded in obtaining the consent of the directors of the Stockton & Darlington Railway Company to an outlay of money for that purpose, which

they trust will enable the committee to extend the benefits of the institution in the way of lectures, classes, and enlarged library.

The committee's half yearly report from mid-1858 gives a further sense of the anticipation surrounding the prospect of a new building:

The S&D Ry Co. have not yet commenced the erection of the new Institute that they have kindly consented to build, but there is every reason to believe that it will be begun as soon as weather, and other circumstances admit, and your Committee will not cease to urge its erection as early as possible, in the mean time we have got the old one repapered and painted and made somewhat comfortable.

The committee is understood to have had a number of schemes placed before them to consider, and the minute books of the fortnightly meetings reveal that a new building was a constant topic of discussion. This continued until we see an entry of particular importance to the Institute's history:

The president reports that the first stone of the new Mechanics Institute was laid on Wednesday, 24th August, 1859.

Now that building work had commenced, the progress was swift. By 10 October that same year, the same President, James Oliver, was reporting that the building had progressed to such a stage that the main exterior structural walls were in place and the roof was ready to be built. Soon afterward he was reporting that fireplaces, gas and water fittings were being installed and that interior plastering was underway.

The site selected for this new dedicated Institute building was part of the town's eastward expansion. Here Station Street was being extended away from the centre of the town and both Victoria Street and Soho Street were added. The new building was erected at the junction where the latest section of Station Street intersected with Cross Street. It overlooked the Stockton and Darlington Railway line and was on an opposite corner to the British School.

The Institute quickly realised that now that they had a premises of their own, it would be necessary to appoint an 'attendant' to look after it, and that such person would require suitable accommodation. Once again they canvassed the railway company, and others in New Shildon. As the building work reached a state of near completion, final arrangements had to be made between the Institute and the owners over the basis under which the new building would be occupied. The directors of the Stockton and Darlington Railway were very charitable in their terms:

> That the building alluded to, belonging this Company at Shildon, be let to that committee at a rental of £1 per annum, and that a suitable agreement be entered into as to the conditions of holding, stipulating that the parties may have immediate possession; that the rental be paid half-yearly; that the Company reserves the right to re-entry on giving the Institute six months notice at any time; that the building be maintained by the committee as long as they have possession in a proper state of repair, except the usual outside repairs which shall be done by the Company; and that the Company by their Agent may at any time inspect the same.

That rental charge of £1 per annum back in 1860 would be roughly the equivalent of £156 at the time of writing this account in 2023. It was a considerably modest fee for the use of a brand new building. The interior of the new premises was revealed to the membership on 17 April 1860, with the formal opening duty being an honour bestowed upon railway company director Henry Pease. Inside the members would find a spacious lecture hall with a raised gallery, two separate smaller rooms, and a small lobby separating the main hall from the main entrance which faced out onto Station Street.

The grand opening went unreported by the, and little is mentioned in any of the report books except to say that the celebratory concert held in the hall was a success. It's written that there was once again such a great attendance that the new hall, with comfortable capacity for four hundred people, was crowded beyond its limits. Many turning up for the event, hoping to get a first glimpse inside the Institute's new home, were consequently turned away. It was estimated that five hundred people had managed to crowd tightly within the building's walls that night. The entertainments were provided by the Sunderland born bandmaster Robert De Lacy and the New Shildon Saxhorn Band that had been formed only a handful of years earlier. Vocal renditions were given by one Mr Marshall, a principal soprano singer with an established reputation, accompanied by a pianist, and the Bishop Auckland Choral Society.

Above: The Institute's first building (centre) on Station Street, which was erected and opened by the Stockton & Darlington Railway Company in 1860.

The artistes, and others, that evening were treated to refreshments, with a total of five shillings having been spent on bread, twenty on cheese and twelve on ale. At the subsequent committee meeting the wisdom and moral basis for provision of alcoholic drinks at the event was retrospectively brought into question.

After the new Institute building had been opened, the committee entered the following text into their half-yearly report:

> We thank the Stockton and Darlington Railway Company in erecting such a noble building as the one we now occupy and which is let to us at a merely nominal rent of £1 per annum. We also thank the Shildon Works Company for their liberality in presenting fittings and furniture for the new hall, classrooms and library.

This new building gave the Institute everything it needed to operate independently instead of relying upon the generous support of the British School and occasional access to other buildings on the railway engineering works site. Furthermore, the committee quickly realised that having their own hall brought potential to make a little money toward their running costs by hiring the new hall to other organisations and groups. They could also host their own fundraising events. Having these new facilities necessitated a revision of the Institute's rules. A new version was drafted, agreed and printed for circulation by mid-summer.

In the meantime, a building attendant had been appointed. This was Jeremiah Bulch, whose son Thomas, a railway fireman, came close to death in 1861, in the same rail accident that readers will remember mentioned in the previous chapter on Thomas MacNay. That accident, a derailment, had occurred between Bowes and Stainmore, and Thomas had spent much of the night scalded, burnt and trapped beneath the stricken locomotive. The rest of the locomotive crew were killed. Thomas narrowly survived and lived to have a son, Thomas Edward, who would become a well known composer of brass music in Shildon and later Australia.

Jeremiah Bulch was around 48 years old when engaged by the Institute and conveniently lived in the house adjacent to the new Institute. This convenience enabled the Institute committee to withdraw their request for suitable accommodation for their attendant.

Almost immediately after taking possession of the hall, those foreseen new opportunities for revenue began to be realised. On 17 April 1860, for example, there was a 'Grand Concert of Vocal and Instrumental Music,' at which a Miss Witham sang. The evening succeeded in raising a considerable sum of five pounds, seven shillings to bolster the Institute's funds. Already enough to cover the first year's rent. On 18 May, the hall was rented for two pounds for another concert featuring Dr Mark and his "Little Men". After that, the New Shildon Saxhorn Band hired the hall for their own concert. These events, and other uses of the hall, breathed new life into the financial prospects of the Institute.

There is evidence that not everything was as orderly as the committee might have wished during these years. A committee report during 1872 expressed frustration with the behaviour of some of the younger members whom it said were tearing newspapers, breaking chairs and talking, to the general annoyance of older members. The serving committee urged their successors to make an example of such offenders.

In February of that same year, the members and committee received the sad news that one of their first benefactors had passed away. At a committee meeting on 4 March 1872 a minute was added to the minute book in tribute:

It is with deep regret that this Committee has to record the death of Mr Joseph Pease, which took place at his residence, Southend, Darlington, Feb 8th 1872. Mr Pease was one of the first patrons of this useful institution, and has encouraged and liberally supported it ever since its commencement. He was greatly instrumental in causing the spacious hall to be erected for the dissemination of useful and intellectual knowledge in Shildon and its vicinity, which deserves to be acknowledged with gratitude and respect. Mr Peases's instructive and edifying lectures on the Holy Land (illustrated with maps and diagrams) delivered in this hall, are well remembered by those who had the privilege of hearing them. Also his eloquent and heart-stirring addresses when advocating the cause of the British and Foreign Bible Society. During his eventful life Mr Pease was the sincere friend of working men, who, by indomitable enterprise and perseverance, opened out fields of industry for them, thereby putting them in a position to help themselves. He was ever ready to promote their social, moral and religious well-being by generous acts of benevolence. The committee desire to record their feeling sympathy with the family of the late lamented gentleman, and to express the high estimation in which he was held by them for many years.

That a copy of this minute be sent to J W Pease Esq., M.P., Hutton Hall, Guisborough and to the Misses pease, Southend, Darlington. Signed, on behalf of the committee, JOHN GLASS, president; WILLIAM DODDS and WILLIAM BAINES, vice-presidents; RICHARD PICKERING, treasurer; GEORGE SHEPHERD, secretary.

Joseph Whitwell Pease wrote back to the Institute on March 12:

So kind, so full, and so sincere a tribute to the memory of my late dear and honoured father is, I can assure you, most acceptable to his family. I should be obliged by your informing your brother office-bearers, the committee, and the members, how truly their expression of sympathy is felt by us all.

Fun and Games

Moving into a new building, and the availability of the several separate rooms there, introduced potential for partaking in new activities and pastimes without disturbing the tranquility of the reading room. Though the committee's report at the end of 1860 bemoaned the members' apathy concerning intellectual improvement, the committee revealed that they had nonetheless introduced some more leisurely pursuits. A draughts board had been carefully painted on the upper surface of a small table placed in one of the two smaller rooms, which thus became designated as a Draughts Room. Both draughts pieces and chess pieces were purchased, enabling both games to be played.

Though draughts was generally played by individuals on an ad-hoc basis, a Draughts Club was founded at the Institute in 1888 with the intention of playing in competition at meetings with other organisations. The Northern Echo of 23 March 1888 tells us a little about one such meeting of draughts players:

> Draughts Match. - A friendly match was played on Tuesday evening by six members of the Shildon District Liberal Club and six members of the New Shildon Mechanics Institute - six games each. The former won eighteen and the latter fourteen games; four draws.

Another report in the North Star of Friday 2 November 1888 tells of a team contest between the Institute and a team from the Bishop Auckland Cocoa Palace Club at which the latter won by eighteen games to nine, with nine games drawn. In March 1890, the Institute's draughts team reached the semi-final of the South Durham and North Yorkshire Draughts Association Challenge Trophy, and played host to Darlington North Road Institute, who they beat by six games to reach the final. Unfortunately they went on to be defeated in that final round by the West Hartlepool Liberal Draughts Club. In one other reported match, taking place on Saturday 29 October 1892, the Institute again hosted a draughts team from its sister Institute at North Road, Darlington, who that time emerged as the eventual victors.

Later in 1878 a new recreation was added; one that would remain popular at the Institute for several decades. This was the game of billiards, a game played on a table similar to a snooker table, with pockets and cues, but using only three balls. Despite having lost popularity in modern times, the game has its origins in the eighteenth century, and proved extremely popular from the mid-nineteenth to mid-twentieth century. A new billiard table was purchased for four pounds, and the members were advised accordingly:

> Your committee have added to the Institute a billiard table for the recreation of members over eighteen years, for which arrangements are about complete, and they hope it may not only be a source of amusement to the members, but also remunerative to the Institution.

As you would expect, the introduction of this new game yielded even more opportunity for competitive bouts between neighbouring organisations. The Northern Echo, on 10 November 1894, describes a meeting between the Institute and the Shildon Liberal Club whereat the first and second billiard teams of the latter club bested their counterparts at the table. A similar report in the Newcastle Daily Chronicle of Saturday 8 Feb 1896 relates a similar outcome, while another in the Northern Echo from Tuesday 28 November 1899 tells of a visit of billiards players from, now familiar local friendly rivals, Darlington North Road Institute. Once more the New Shildonians were defeated.

Such contests became increasingly formal. We know that in 1895 the North Eastern Railway Institutes at York, Newcastle and Darlington inaugurated inter-Institute Billiard Competitions with a cup and league to compete for. The Shildon institute joined these organised competitions a little later than the other Institutes. The contest was so successful in attracting new membership to the four participating Institutes that by 1901 the respective committees felt able to contribute toward a silver cup. This cost around 12 guineas, and the intention was that the winning Institute each year would retain it for the remainder of the year. The Institute at Darlington were to prove the dominant cup winners throughout the first thirteen years of that competition. In 1902 Darlington were crowned eventual champions over the other three Institutes after what was declared an easy final win against the Shildon Institute on 15 March. An additional fifth Institute, the Forth Institute at Newcastle, was admitted to the contest from 1909.

The use of playing cards at the Institute was handled with a little more caution by the committee. This was due to fears that the members would use them to resort to gambling, which of course, if you recall the incident involving the frying pocket watches, was an act very much contrary to the Institute' principles. The committee eventually made a concession to members in December 1898 that it would purchase three packs of playing cards, and that card games would be allowed, as an experiment. Only members over twenty-one years of age were permitted to play, and the hours in which such games could be played were limited to between six and ten in the evening, or two o'clock in the afternoon until half-past-ten on Saturdays. Naturally a number of members reportedly flouted these rules and there were instances of covert gambling. The committee are reported to have dealt firmly with anyone brought to their attention.

In 1900, the four principal North Eastern Railway Institutes commenced a whist competition, and the Shildon Institute would demonstrate far more success at this game than they had at billiards. Teams of eight whist players from each Institute met at the same time as the Billiard players. A shield trophy was purchased in 1904 to be offered as a prize. The Shildon Institute won this in 1904, 1905 and in 1911.

In time, more physical sports were adopted by members under the Institute's banner. We know that a football team was formed in the early 1890s. The first evidential clue being a mention the Institute's Minute Book in an entry from 6 November 1893 where it was resolved:

> That the committee of the Institute recognise the Football Club in connection with the Institute's members and allow the use of rooms for meetings, dressing, etc.

It's not clear whether that team participated in any league during its earliest years, but there were certainly other teams in the area with whom they might compete, and we do know that it took part in local tournament competitions. One particular occasion, on Saturday 4 September 1897, the Institute's football eleven took to the field to compete in a tournament at Redworth that had been organised in connection with that village's annual sports day. They were one of only four teams competing, the others being Auckland Park, Darlington Rangers and Middridge. The latter of those teams won the tournament, and its players received silver medals as prizes.

Naturally, a cricket team was also eventually formed in association with the Institute. A meeting minute captured on 15 June 1897 explained how £2 was to be given from the Institute's funds toward the Institute's young men's Athletic Club for cricket equipment. Shortly afterward reports began to emerge in the press of that team competing with other cricket teams in the locality in what were described as 'ordinary' matches, which were presumably leisurely challenge matches rather than relating to a league or tournament. One report in the North Star newspaper, which was edited and printed in Darlington, tells of a cricket match at Heighington where the young men of the Institute beat their local opposition with a score of 131 runs to 45. Another in that same newspaper, but this time in 1907, indicates that the Institute had sufficient players for a second eleven, as it tells of a victory over a team from Croft where the Institute's second string scored 107 runs for Croft's 21. On Saturday 12 June 1909, both the first and second teams from the Institute played their counterparts at Houghton-le-Skerne, and in June did so again with Harrowgate Hill as opponents. Whenever the cricketing first team were playing on their home ground, the second string would play away, and vice-versa.

In the early part of that century a cricket ground was created for the Institute's cricket team at the western end of the Shildon Works site.

A team registered in association with the Institute in 1913 played in the Mid-Durham Senior Cricket League. Following the merger of the North Eastern Railway into the London North Eastern Railway in 1923, this team played as Shildon LNER Cricket Club.

Cricket continued to be a pivotal part of the Institute's sports offering through to the late Twentieth Century when these sporting activities were separated from the interests of the Institute by events that we shall arrive at later. We'll also return to more cricketing achievements in later chapters.

Worthy and Inspiring Portraits

Returning to 1969, and the Institute at Station Street, in August the committee and members received, with great sadness, news from Darlington that its most revered first Secretary, Thomas MacNay, had passed away at his home. MacNay, had been such a stout champion and supporter of the Stockton & Darlington Railway's supported Institutes after having written the original manifesto of the first one at New Shildon. His passing was much lamented by those who knew him.

The committee expressed a wish to procure and display a portrait of MacNay in the Lecture Hall. This desire was duly fulfilled, though it took until 14 October 1871 to acquire the portrait. This became the first of what would, over subsequent decades, gradually become an impressive collection depicting esteemed gentlemen with a connection to both locality and Institute. These portraits were mounted upon the walls of the Lecture Hall as a source of inspiration, and perhaps expectation, for the promising young men of the area.

At some point in the twentieth century this collection was, sadly, disposed of, with many of the portraits making their way into the hands of national museum collections. We know that some are today held by the Science Museum. Consequently, visitors to the Institute today are unable to enjoy them here. Despite this we do have enough written and photographic evidence to know quite a lot about which portraits were held by the Institute, what some looked like and where some were later displayed.

The acquisition of some of the portraits was recorded in Institute report and minute books, though not all of them. Also, in the mid 1920s, while writing his account of Timothy Hackworth's life and achievements as a locomotive engineer for his biographical book, the author, Robert Young, looking for suitable illustrations, wrote to the Institute to find out what pictures they might have. He received a reply from Francis Bainbridge itemising the portraits held by the Institute. Young acquired images of some of the portraits, and included them in his book, attributing source ownership to the Institute. That book became the most thorough account of the life of Timothy Hackworth yet written, and was entitled "Timothy Hackworth and the Locomotive."

Volunteers at the Institute have collated this information and other evidence to create a list of portraits that are known to have once adorned the walls of the Institute.

Subject	Format	Acquired
Daniel Adamson	Engraving	1875
William Bouch	Engraving	1875
Henry W F Bolckow	Engraving	not known
Francis P Cockshott	Engraving	1875
Sir David Dale	Engraving	not known
Edward Fletcher	Engraving	1875
John Graham	Photograph	not known
George Graham	Photograph	not known
John Glass	Painting	not known
Timothy Hackworth	Painting	1876
Joseph Pease	Painting	not known
Edward A Pease	Engraving	1876
Arthur Pease	Engraving	1876
Joseph Whitwell Pease	Engraving	1874
Henry Pease	Engraving	1876
Richard Pickering	Engraving	1882

John Pickering		1875
Charles Mark Palmer MP	Engraving	1874
Alfred Kitching	Engraving	not known
R Newton	Engraving	not known
Col. Henry Stobart	Engraving	1873
Henry Tennant	Engraving	1875
D S Foster	Engraving	not known
F W Worsdell	Engraving	not known
G W Wilkinson	Engraving	not known
G P Wilkinson	Engraving	not known
Joseph Dodds	Engraving	1875
Mr Howe	Painting	not known
A Lincoln	Engraving	not known
Mr Johnson	Engraving	not known
Rev. James Manisty	Photograph	not known
John Marley	Photograph	1886
Thomas MacNay	Photograph	1871
James Raper	Photograph	1874
Thomas Barlow	Photograph	1876
Sir William Chaytor	Etching	1882
Thomas Greener	Painting	1874
S Marley	Photograph	not known
Edmund Backhouse MP	(unknown)	1874
J L Hopkins	(unknown)	1874
Rev. Horatio Spurrier	(unknown)	1874
Alfred Robson	(unknown)	1876
Robert Morton	(unknown)	1876
William Dale Trotter	(unknown)	1876

To those who know of the North East of England's industrial heritage in the nineteenth century, the list above reads like a star studded cast of industrialists, engineers, coal owners, politicians clergy and investors, though it does of course include a handful of persons only relevant to the history of the Institute itself. You might have seen some of these names already in this small history, while others will appear later. The list features several generations of the Pease family, whose influence brought New Shildon into being. Four of those named on the list are sufficiently well known in the town to have had streets named after them.

If the people in these portraits were intended to inspire the younger members of the Institute, then perhaps they should. A fair proportion of these local personalities had not been born into positions of privilege. They could be considered self-made men, who had taken the opportunities and facilities presented to them and used those to elevate themselves to respected positions. We have already read, for example, of Daniel Adamson, the bright young man who used his experiences as apprentice to Hackworth to set up his own industry in Manchester. Now let's take a look at another example.

Francis Pickersgill Cockshott (1824-1896)

Francis Cockshott was born on 14 April 1824 in Addingham, Yorkshire to parents William and Dorothy. An obituary following his death explained that Francis, as a young man, remembered meetings between Edward Pease and George Stephenson regarding the Stockton & Darlington Railway at the Pease's office in Darlington, though these would not have been the earliest meetings relating to that railway as Cockshott would not have been born when those took place.

Above: Francis Pickersgill Cockshott, at one time a Shildon Works clerk and Institute member who became a respected Railway Superintendent and whose portrait was displayed to inspire younger members.

He went to work for Joseph Pease MP in 1841 when the latter was Treasurer of the Stockton & Darlington Railway Company. From 22 October 1845 he was apprenticed as a clerk at the Shildon Works. We know that Francis had some direct interaction with the Institute while an employee of the S&DR. For example, he delivered a lecture on Teesdale in 1848. He may also have been a relative of the F Cockshott who had been present at the founding of the Institute in 1833.

Francis's keen abilities and direct experience with the Stockton & Darlington Railway Company eventually earned him a job as Goods Manager of the Edinburgh, Perth and Dundee line in Scotland. He married Jane Anne Dobson, in Darlington, in 1850.

Having then demonstrated himself to be a diligent and capable manager, he was promoted to Railway Superintendent. Before the end of 1851, he had moved on yet again, this time to the southern end of the country where he was appointed to the post of Traffic Manager by the South Devon Railway. His responsibilities increased further in 1858, when the South Devon merged with the Cornwall Railway, bringing traffic there under his control.

It was while he was acting in this capacity that Pickersgill was put in charge of the opening of Isambard Kingdom Brunel's rather unique Royal Albert Bridge between Plymouth and Saltash in 1859, which spanned a total of almost 2,188 feet across the River Tamar. This grand opening was conducted in the presence of Albert, Prince Consort to Queen Victoria.

In 1865, Cockshott rose yet again, to the prestigious post of Traffic Superintendent of the Great Northern Railway, becoming responsible for main line traffic to the North. While carrying out this job he gained an excellent reputation for ensuring punctuality.

His wife, Jane died on 7 June 1890. Francis himself retired in December 1895, and passed away aged 71, on 17 February 1896 at 32 Carlton Road, Tufnell Park, Islington, Middlesex. He left a significant estate of almost £68,000.

By 1875 when his portrait was acquired by the Institute at Shildon, Cockshott had become just the kind of fellow the committee there wanted young men to contemplate, look up to and aspire to emulate.

A collection of papers, that included personal letters, forms of apprenticeship, appreciations of his work and letters of condolence to his family after his death were donated to the National Archives in 1961 by his grand-daughters. These donated effects included an illuminated address signed by over 100 persons, gifted to him on his retirement. It illustrated perfectly the high esteem in which he was held, and how far he had come since being apprenticed at Shildon.

Other Institute Societies and Meetings

Having a new building at their complete disposal presented much more than simply opportunities for the Institute and its members. Just as the Institute had once relied upon the accommodation of others for meetings, lectures and events, it now had the opportunity to provide similar facility for other societies.

The minute books maintained by the committee captured the dates on which a number of other societies approached them to make use of, or start something new at, the Institute's hall.

One of the first to take advantage was a Shildon Choral Society, which according to minutes held its inaugural meeting at the hall on 5 August 1861. There is some ambiguity around this, as we have also seen contradictory evidence that there was a New Shildon Choral Society three years previous. In November 1858 they arranged for a grand choral concert in one of the Soho Works buildings with proceeds going toward the Wesleyan Chapel. It may be, however, that the original group disbanded and the minute referred to a reforming of the society, or even that there were several attempts to form a Choral Society. There is additional evidence to support this theory, including a report in the Hartlepool Northern Daily Mail of 10 March 1886 which told of an inaugural concert by a society of the same name in the Institute hall the evening before. Reports of events held under the auspices of that society at the Institute hall continued for several years thereafter.

On 4 November 1861 the Society of Friends, better known to most nowadays as the Quakers, held an inaugural meeting at the Institute. Other religious movements also came forward in subsequent years. 29 February 1864, for example, saw an inaugural meeting of the Church of England, All Saints, with the Reverend W Hitchcock present. This is especially interesting in that it was probably the beginning of meetings to plan the erection of the new church for the town of New Shildon. A history of All Saints church, written in 1968 to commemorate its centenary, tells us that a committee of railway officials, landowners and other interested parties was formed in 1866 to launch a building fund, but these minutes from the Institute records suggest that discussions were being held much earlier. Perhaps the recorded meetings were just to plan the creation of that committee.

What's also interesting is that as part of the new church committee's appeal for money, John Scott the third Earl of Eldon granted two acres of land upon which the church and vicarage could be built, as well as a financial contribution of £500. It has been claimed in histories of the building that the church was named All Saints as a consequence of this generous gift, the connection being that All Saints Day was the closest saints day to the Earl's birthday of 8 November. Yet as we can see, the group that met in 1864 had already chosen the name All Saints. Had the Earl promised his land contribution much earlier?

1854 also saw an inaugural meeting of the Congregational Church at the Institute. Decades later, in May 1897, a similar meeting was held in the Institute hall by members of the Roman Catholic Church, keen to establish a presence in the town under the Reverend Father Little.

It was not only the religious bodies that sought to use the Institute hall as a springboard to establish a presence in the town. Other societies either hired the hall, or else used it to set up their new societies. In 1863 a Shildon Anti-Tobacco Society and associated Penny Savings Bank were established, with a view to dissuading smoking and further showing the benefits of quitting by demonstrating how much money could be saved.

Benefit societies, a key source of support for the working classes prior to the introduction of the Welfare State, were also holding their meetings at the Institute. These were organisations to which workers could subscribe, contributing a small regular amount from their wages to a common fund from which payments could be drawn if and when they then encountered an hour of need. For example, the Locomotive Enginemen and Firemen's Benefit Society, New Shildon Branch, held a meeting at the Institute in April 1894. At that gathering, a report was given concerning changes in the rules of that society that had resulted from its national conference. The changes included a clause that engine cleaners could now become members at half-rate until they achieve promotion to firemen; another that the rate of sickness benefit had been reduced to ten shillings per week for twenty-six weeks, and a final change that the death allowance had been reduced, largely as a consequence of the volume of claims being received.

Some of the meetings held at the Institute were for political purposes. In the mid-nineteenth century the only people in the country that had the right to vote in a General Election were men that owned land and property. Women were completely denied the right to vote. There had been a prevailing belief among the among the wealthy that the working classes were not deserving of a vote. Some no doubt feared the consequences of what might happen to their own power, prospects and privileges if that right were extended. However in 1866, following the death of Lord Palmerston who had fiercely argued against reform, Earl Russell introduced a reform bill proposing that 'respectable' working men should be given 'the franchise'.

Such working men would have to be paying at least seven pounds annually in rent to be deemed suitably 'respectable'. Nonetheless the introduction of the bill would have represented a significant advance toward the enfranchisement of workers.

Alas, the Parliamentary vote on the bill created a significant split within Russell's ruling Liberal Party. A sufficient enough proportion of the Whigs voted with the Conservative Party against the bill to result in its defeat. This failure to pass the bill also caused the failure of Russell's government and they were forced to resign. They were replaced by a Conservative led government under Benjamin Disraeli. In the midst of this sequence of events, on Tuesday 3 April 1866 a meeting was held at the New Shildon Mechanics Institute to raise a petition to present to Parliament expressing that the meeting viewed "with indignation the opposition, especially by professed Liberals, to the reform bill".

Clearly rejecting the bill was seen as contrary to the interests of the working men of New Shildon, and they weren't afraid to say so. A further motion was passed to request that their MP, then Joseph Whitwell Pease, would present the resulting petition to Parliament, and that support should also be requested from Henry Surtees, the Conservative candidate in opposition, then resident at Redworth Hall.

Despite the rejection of the bill, the seeds of electoral reform had been sown, and were germinating. Pressure continued to mount across the nation. Disraeli introduced a Reform Act of his own in 1866, which received Royal Assent in 1867. The following year another General Election was held. One in which those 'respectable' working men became able to cast their vote for the first time. The outcome was defeat for Disraeli and his Tories, and a Liberal government under William Gladstone.

The committee of the Institute were not always amenable to letting the hall. In May 1873 a request was submitted by a Pastor Gordon who planned to deliver a lecture on the Principles of Liberation Society. This was an organisation with a core belief in the disestablishment of the Church of England. The committee of the Institute refused his request, fearing that the planned meeting would result in public order disturbances, such as had happened at a similar meeting in Bishop Auckland a short time before. Gordon's meeting in the Shildons did still take place, but having been turned down by other organisations with premises, it took place in the open air, in the market place at Old Shildon.

Both of the main local political parties of the day held meetings at the Institute, canvassing the support and votes of the newly enfranchised working men. On Tuesday 6 January 1885, for example, the South Durham Conservative Association hired the hall and offered the platform to several speakers. Henry Surtees chaired the meeting, but was supported by his prominent local sympathiser, the vicar of Old Shildon, Horatio Spurrier.

Later in November of that same year it was James Mellor Paulton, the Liberal candidate for the new Bishop Auckland Parliamentary Division, that held court at the Institute. This meeting reportedly saw the hall so crowded that many were unable to get through the doors. Paulton emerged victorious in the 1885 General Election, becoming that constituency's first MP. He was sufficiently well thought of by the Institute committee for his portrait to have been hung upon the wall with the others.

Liberals continued to hold occasional political meetings at the Institute throughout the remainder of the nineteenth century. Conservatives had a very long wait to achieve electoral success in Bishop Auckland, with their first successful candidate being elected only recently, in 2019. Meetings of other smaller political parties were held there too. In 1889 Arthur Pease held a meeting there as part of his campaign while standing as a Unionist candidate. This was before his later campaigns which led to him being elected as a Liberal MP, first for Whitby, and then later Darlington.

Political meetings at the Institute were not only those organised by parliamentary parties. Some were organised by the workers of New Shildon themselves.

In the 1870s, trade unionism was in the ascendency, and in 1871, with the support of a Liberal MP, Michael Thomas Bass, an industrial union was founded to give a collective voice and representation to railway workers. It was entitled the Amalgamated Society of Railway Servants or ASRS. In its early years the organisation found recruitment challenging, partly due to the formation of several other parallel trade unions. All were competing to form the strongest body to represent the railwaymen.

As an incentive to join the trade unions, like Friendly Societies, the unions established forms of hardship fund to support their members in their times of need. On Sunday 13 July 1890 the Bishop of Durham, Dr Westcott, attended a service and meeting of the Amalgamated Society of Railway Servants at the Institute, with a view to promoting its Orphan Fund. After the meeting a procession followed the New Shildon Temperance Band over the railway footbridge and up the hill to All Saints Church for a sermon on the subject of "brotherhood", an appropriate theme for a day organised with a trade unionism in mind. The Amalgamated Society of Railway Servants continued to meet at the Institute throughout the 1890s and beyond before ultimately merging as part of the National Union of Railwaymen in 1913. They used the meetings to campaign on a range of issues including promoting the movement to introduce an eight-hour working day for rail workers.

Developments at Station Street

The members and committee gradually began to experience a number of issues with the Mechanics Institute building on Station Street. It is perhaps surprising how soon these began to emerge. During 1866, when the building was only six years old, the committee noticed defects in the roof of the building. They recommended to the members that the building be closed temporarily, for safety, while they brought the matter to the attention of the railway company. The latter attended to necessary repairs, while the Institute members made kind use of the hospitality of the British School once again.

By 1873 the members were concerned once again over the overall suitability of the building, and had a few thoughts and suggestions as to how it might be improved. The Secretary's report for that year says:

> Your committee would urge upon their successors the desirability of taking immediate steps towards having the Hall altered, so as to make the place more comfortable, provide better accommodation for the members and enable the committee to carry on the classes for the Institute.

The Institute had improved upon what it offered to the community around it, through the provision of new classes and activities. In response, the membership had swollen to even greater numbers. Francis Bainbridge, in his centenary book, tells us that the Institute's reading room had become too small for the readers to read in comfort, and that the playing of billiards was often prevented on account of the hall needing to be used for other purposes. These difficulties carried on, with frequent representations being made to the board of the North Eastern Railway Company, as latest building owners, for help. Those requests bore fruit when, in 1885, a significant upgrade to the Institute was implemented.

The Institute building was closed for two months during that year while some alterations were made. The railway company had acquired the house adjacent to the Institute, and modified it to create a considerable extension which now included a larger reading room and a separate billiard room. The newly reconfigured and adjoined buildings were re-opened on Monday 28 September, almost sixty years to the day after the opening of the Stockton and Darlington Railway.

Above: In 1885 the Institute hall on Station Street, which once stood in what is now the gap on the left, was expanded to annex this house (right) which still stands today. It was also once the home of the first Institute caretaker.

Joseph Whitwell Pease MP, being also a Director of the railway company, presided over the re-opening ceremony. He gave recollections of Timothy Hackworth, praising his studiousness and achievements. He also recalled his old friends William Bouch, and Thomas MacNay, and their respective roles in the Institute's history. He spoke too of Daniel Adamson who had received instruction through the Institute, and of John Glass, another champion of the organisation.

The NER's Locomotive Superintendent, Thomas William Worsdell, and David Dale, also addressed those present at the re-opening, after which tea was served and a musical entertainment was given by a band under the conductorship of Mr Robert Bowron, who had once been bandmaster of the New Shildon Philharmonic Band, and was a fine pianist and singer. As always the event had been made possible through the ardent efforts of several ladies of the town who were thanked in the committee's half-yearly report at the end of that year.

This new extension, once it had been floored with linoleum and furnished, was deemed sufficiently good to warrant the purchase of a new billiard table, for the substantial sum of fifty-eight pounds, ten shillings and sixpence.

John Glass - Long Serving President

One of the people Joseph Pease saw fit to mention in his 1885 address, mentioned above, was John Glass, who is a particularly notable figure in the history of the early years of the Institute. He had been born in 1810 at Upleatham near Redcar. When the Stockton & Darlington Railway Company was commencing its work in 1822, John's father was awarded a contract for the creation of a small portion of the line. Young John, then only twelve years old, had been present when the first rail was laid by Thomas Meynell.

John worked alongside his father, and was fortunate enough to have been a passenger on that first steam hauled train that had left Brusselton Bank Foot for Stockton on 27 September 1825. He was also present at the grand banquet held at Darlington in 1875 to commemorate the fiftieth anniversary of that occasion.

John had also been present at the formation of the Institute in 1833, at which time he would have been twenty-three years of age. He remained a servant and champion of its services ever after. He became the Station Master at the somewhat crude New Shildon Station from 1834, and the much improved one that had been built after the Prince of Wales Tunnel opened in 1842. After 1854 he became a Mineral Agent for the railway company, and during this period lived at Thickley Cottage.

Glass was the Institute's longest serving President, having fulfilled that position during two periods. The first time for two years between 1861 and 1863, and the second a further seventeen years between 1867 and his death - a total of nineteen years overall.

During that time he published at least two booklets. The first was an address delivered to the Etherley Mechanics Institute on New Year's Eve of 1849, where, in the presence of eminent coal owner Henry Stobart, he extolled the virtues of Mechanics Institutes and spoke of their successes as well as an outline of the life and character of pioneering engineer George Stephenson.

Above: Portrait of John Glass, Mineral Agent of Shildon who was also the longest serving President of the Institute at Shildon.
From a portrait once held by the Institute.

The following extract from that speech tells us something of Glass's outlook on life, the interaction between classes, and the Institutes he held dear:

Mechanics' Institutions are bringing together different classes of society, and I venture to say that neither the gentry nor the clergy lose one iota of the respect due to their station in life by mingling with the working classes on such occasions as the present. I hope they will always be treated with due respect not with superfluous formality, or excess of ceremony, but in a decent and becoming manner; it is all a gentleman requires who is in reality a gentleman in every sense of the word, and he ought not to be treated a with less. An industrious working man should never be bashful, and hang down his head in the presence of his superiors; it is beneath a free born Briton to be afraid of any man.

The second booklet Glass wrote, in 1875, was an account of the life of Thomas Greener, telling of his life in the service of the Stockton & Darlington Railway, working as Engineman at the static engine house at the top of the Etherley railway incline. It was entitled "A Railway Engineer of 1825." As President of the Institute, John Glass took an interest in every aspect of its day to day running and governance, and was active in sharing his knowledge and experience with younger members. In 1860, for example, he addressed the New Shildon Institute, delivering a lecture on the Progress of the Railways.

When he died, on Christmas Eve 1884, it was claimed in the newspapers that up until his death, John Glass was among the oldest, if he was not the oldest, living railway employee in the world. A fairly bold claim given that the Stockton and Darlington Railway, though the first steam hauled passenger railway, was not the oldest railway by any means. It would have been fairer and more accurate to say the he was oldest former S&DR employee at the time. He had spent sixty-two years of his life in the service of the two railway companies. Around the time of his death he was said to have been planning a retirement that, quite sadly, he was never granted time to enjoy.

Considered a much respected man throughout his lifetime, he had also served as the Chairman of the British Schools Committee, and was a stout advocate of the value of good education.

A Class of Their Own

Another benefit of having a dedicated Institute building was gaining capacity to host a regular educational offering. It now had access to a classroom sized space that could be used as such whenever the organisation wished to do so, rather than having to seek a large room elsewhere.

The Institute in the late Victorian period was operating in an era before the introduction of a National Health Service. It was also located in a heavy industrial engineering town in which accidents were to be expected. It is consequently unsurprising that ambulance classes, which taught basic medical aid for a variety of injuries, were held, and also assessed, at the Institute. An article in the Northern Echo in February 1891 tells of one such examination:

> On Saturday, an ambulance class of North Eastern Railway men was examined at the Mechanics' Institute, New Shildon by Dr Ellerton of Middlesbrough. The class had been instructed by Dr Ratcliff-Gaylard, and in a short address to the candidates at the conclusion of the examination the examiner expressed himself as being thoroughly satisfied.

Practical first aid was certainly a useful skill set to have, and the large railway works would certainly have need of the skills of those so trained. The success of the ambulance classes in New Shildon may also have been partly responsible for the fact that after the breakout of the First World War in 1914, many of the recruits enlisting from Shildon workforce found themselves in the ranks of the Royal Army Medical Corps, rescuing wounded soldiers from battlefields on several fronts. The works continued to operate ambulance classes and keep its own ambulance vehicles right up to its closure in the 1980s.

In 1885, enabled by the expansion to the Institute's building, the Institute commenced another programme of classes, this time in Science and in Art. In order to commence this activity, the Institute applied for, and secured, grants to fund the cost of tuition. In the first year the grant was £38, and within ten years it had increased to £191. Across those first ten years the whole grant money secured had been over £675, and for that money they had been able to educate 508 students in total. On 2 October 1895 a meeting was held, with Rev Henry Greene in the chair, to celebrate these successes. The results of that year's May exams were presented, and a concert was given by the Shildon Orchestral Society. Works by the students were exhibited on the walls of the hall. Reverend Greene and others presented prizes to students at an annual prize-giving ceremony also held at the Institute.

Above: Rev. Henry Greene did a tremendous amount of work to introduce Science and Art classes at the Institute in the late Victorian era. Sketch portrait from an obituary in the Evening Chronicle, Newcastle 13 July 1906.

Greene was born on 13 Dec 1842, in Bingley, Yorkshire, and graduated in 1871 with a Bachelor of Arts from St John's College, Cambridge. In 1875 he attained a Master of Arts qualification. He subsequently became a vociferous champion of the virtues of a good education. He was ordained a deacon in 1870, and became a priest in 1871. His career in the clergy took him to St John's Church in Huddersfield, St Luke's in Middlestown, St Cuthbert's in Southport before he arrived at All Saints Church in New Shildon. Here he served between 1883 and 1898. For eleven of his fourteen years in New Shildon he was the chairman of the Art and Science Classes committee there. He was a founder of the Clergy Pension Institution and also fond of literary work, contributing to several religious and home journals and magazines. In addition to this he authored several pamphlets on humanitarian values. After his time at All Saints Church, Henry Greene went on to become Vicar of St John the Baptist Church in Newcastle-upon-Tyne, where he remained until his death at the vicarage on Summerhill Terrace on 12 July 1906. He was buried at Elswick Cemetery.

As time progressed, the classes at the Institute were increasingly held with the co-operation of the National Schools, in both Old and New Shildon, and the British School across the street from the Institute. Many of the subjects covered were selected to be of distinct practical value, and interestingly were also opened to female students. Some subjects had even been specifically included to help them into occupations deemed appropriate for young ladies. A report from 1897 explained how, that year, fifty students had availed themselves of the art classes, thirty-five pursued machine construction and drawing, six took mathematics, five studied applied mechanics, nine studied electricity, four geometry and sixty dressmaking.

The ambulance classes we spoke of earlier continued to be held at the Institute after the organisation moved to a new premises at Redworth Road, a change which we will arrive at shortly. In June 1915 it was reported in the North Eastern Railway Magazine how such classes had taken place there, whereafter certificates had been handed out to the successful students by Robert William Worsdell, a Manager at the North Eastern Railway Company, along with Doctor Robert Smeddle, the lecturer in charge of the classes. The latter was also presented with a pipe and cigarette holder, each with separate cases, as a mark of appreciation. At a similar event in 1918, where class members were presented with certificates, medallions and labels, Dr Smeddle received a pocket wallet from Mr Worsdell as a gesture of thanks for running the classes.

The Gift of Stephenson's Letter

In 1903 a gift was presented to the Institute by a Mr Hodgson Watson of London, which was mounted and framed and put on prominent display at the Institute. This was a letter from the railway and civil engineer George Stephenson to Timothy Hackworth. The letter read:

"Liverpool, July 25, 1828.

Dear Timothy,

Brandreth has given a report that you are going to lay off the locomotive engines. Is it so? It was a great pity that these accidents took place with the tubes. It appears Brandreth has got my plan introduced for the horses to ride, which I suppose he will set off as his own invention. It is more than two years since I explained this to Brandreth. Canterbury was the place where I meant to have it put to use, but as that company have now determined to work the line by steam power it will not be wanted. We have tried the new locomotive engine at Bolton, which works beautifully. There is not the least noise about it. We have also tried the blast to it for burning coke, and I believe it will answer. There were two bellows worked by eccentrics underneath the tender. The line will be opened on August 1. Is it too far for you to come or should I be glad to see you. Write me about the engines by return of post if you can. Yours truly, GEO STEPHENSON.

PS. John Dixon and other directors at Canterbury can speak of my plan of carrying horses, which I mentioned to them two years ago, but I never considered it ought to be tried at Darlington as then I considered the locomotive engines a better thing. - G.S."

The Walsall Observer of Saturday 21 Feb 1903 carried a story about the gift, noting that on the letter mount was a sketch of Hackworth's locomotive, Royal George, the Stockton & Darlington Railway Company's No. 5 locomotive which had been built to Hackworth's own design at New Shildon and tried in September 1827. It was the first to use Hackworth's invention of the steam blast pipe and, as we explained earlier, the first locomotive to prove that steam locomotive power really could be more economical and efficient than using horses to haul coal.

Quite how Hodgson Watson had come into possession of this letter is unclear. Nowadays it is referred to as the "blast pipe" letter, and often cited as evidence that the innovation was Hackworth's invention. Robert Young's book "Timothy Hackworth and the Locomotive" published in 1923, made reference to the letter and included a transcript. We know that Young received assistance from the Institute's Francis Bainbridge, and we know that this historically important letter was still at the Institute at that time. We know that this letter did not remain with the Institute, and the Institute retains a document explaining what happened to it.

It is through the content of another letter held in the Institute's own collection of archive material that we know where the historically important letter went, though this does not state why. The "blast pipe" letter was handed over to the Durham County Record Office on 16 December 1968. The following day the county's archivist wrote the a letter to the Institute acknowledging receipt and conditions under which it may be returned:

"Dear Mr Brabban,

I am writing to acknowledge formally receipt of the framed letter from George Stephenson to Timothy Hackworth, 1828, and the volume on 'Timothy Hackworth and the Locomotive' by R Young, 1923, both of which I collected from you last night. These have been accepted for deposit in the County Record Office on the understanding that, if they should ever be required, they will only be returned on the receipt of a request by the Secretary for the time being of the British Rail Staff Institute at Shildon.

As I said when I spoke to you last night I shall always be pleased to accept on the same terms any other records such as Committee Minutes, balance sheets etc. relating to the activities of the Institute in the past.

Yours sincerely,

W A L Seaman
County Archivist"

From the Durham County Archives we know that somehow the letter then made its way into the hands of the National Railway Museum, where it now forms part of the Joan Hackworth-Weir collection. It could be questioned whether the Durham County Archives should have handed it on, given the terms of their tenure as described in their letter, but it does appear to be an appropriate home for such a significant document.

Courts and Inquiries

Again, as a consequence of the Institute acquiring its own

dedicated, though rented, building, it was able to become a convenient location for other formal or official meetings that needed to be held in the community. For example, it was an ideal venue for coroners to hold inquiries into deaths that had taken place in the locality. It also met all the criteria necessary for holding somewhat curious sessions that went by the name of Revision Courts.

These were sessions where, in the presence of officials from the principal political parties, the Conservatives and the Liberals, decisions were made as to whether certain persons should be excluded from the Electoral Rolls. Can you imagine such a thing today? Naturally, both main parties were highly interested in this process as it might influence their chances of retaining or gaining their Parliamentary seat at Westminster.

In one such Revision Court session, on Thursday 6 September 1894 the Revising Barrister overseeing the process was Mr Charles Haigh, Barrister-at-Law, whose job was to adjudicate on the voter lists for Eldon, Middridge, Middridge Grange, Shildon, East Thickley and Windlestone.

Within that session a case was being made for the ineligibility of the Reverend W Johnston, a Methodist minister with Conservative sympathies, of which the report in the Northern Echo claimed there were few. The Liberal Party representatives claimed that Mr Johnson had moved to Shildon too recently and therefore had not served the qualifying period to vote. Mr Johnson countered this claim by saying that though he had not moved to his home in Shildon in time, his ministry had commenced earlier than he had arrived so he should still be eligible. The barrister ruled that the claim of the Liberals was 'bad' and the Liberals agreed to withdraw their objection to Mr Johnson's vote.

This was but one case handled in a single session of claims, reclaims and objections that ultimately saw a shift in voter eligibility to the advantage of the Liberals. At the end of the session they consulted the barrister on the competence of the Overseer of the Electoral Roll for Shildon, a Mr Fryer, on the basis that he had struck off so many of the working men that the barrister had subsequently reinstated. Mr Linday, representing the Liberals, questioned whether Mr Fryer's payment for overseeing the list ought to be withheld, though the barrister gave the Overseer the benefit of the doubt, claiming him to be a stranger in the division.

It does seem remarkably strange in current times, when individuals qualify to vote in national and regional elections simply on the basis of age and whether they are registered to vote, that in those days, during which the right to vote was tied to gender and the ownership of property, that the political parties wrangled with each other at the New Shildon Institute over whether people should be granted or denied their right.

Of the coroners inquiries, so many examples are reported in those newspapers of the day that it might be interesting to take a look at a handful to capture a sense of the kind of investigation taking place. For example, on Tuesday 21 May 1895, the coroner, Mr Proud, held an inquest at the Institute regarding the death of John Robert Atkinson, who was aged only one year and eight months. His death was the result of a terrible accident. His mother had placed a kettle of boiled water on the floor, and the child had fallen over it, resulting in the boiled water splashing all over him and scalding his body. This produced the injuries from which he died. The inquest jury returned a verdict that the death was accidental.

In March 1902, Coroner Proud held an inquest into the death of on George Bell, aged 37, a music master of Cockton Hill in Bishop Auckland who had been killed travelling by rail at Simpasture just outside Shildon. It was thought that he had been caught by the bridge there whilst leaning out of the carriage window to look. James Woodward, chief assistant to the Darlington District Engineer, had presented evidence that blood and hair had been found on the stonework of the bridge. The blow had been so severe that the victim was pulled from the carriage. Again the inquest jury returned a verdict of accidental death.

Other examples brought before that coroner, or his deputy, Mr F Badcock, at the Institute included 64 year-old blacksmith Thomas Marrs, of 14 Soho Street, who was deemed to have drowned himself in a three feet deep pond in 1903; Mrs Fearne, aged 26, of Strand Street, who poisoned herself to death with mouse-poison and Richard Bellwood, a wagon repairer of Beresford Street who had hanged himself in his scullery in 1906. All of these were declared as having committed suicide during temporary insanity.

Another sad case brought before the coroner at the Institute was that of the death of the one-year-old child of James Moss. The baby had been wearing a flannelette gown which it seems had caught fire being too close to the fireplace. His mother had come into the room to find the child ablaze upon the burning hearth rug. The inquest jury ruled that the death was due to shock as a result of the burns accidentally received.

Industrial Action and a New Building

By the end of the nineteenth century, it was clear that the Institute building on Station Street was worn, tired, past its best and beginning to show signs of structural defects. On 3 December 1900, a sub-committee was appointed consisting of Messrs Pick, Lowthian, Bland, Dr Smeddle, and the Institute secretary. Their appointed task was to draw up a letter appealing to Sir Joseph Whitwell Pease and Sir David Dale with regard to their promise of a new Institute building for New Shildon. Their reaction was to be slow in coming. On 4 December 1906 a further report of the committee read:

> The Secretary reported cracks in the walls of the Institute, and after some discussion this matter was left to Mr Pick to deal with.

Subsequently on 2 April 1906 it was decided that the Institute Hall should be closed entirely, and that the secretary was to communicate this decision to those who occupy it regularly. The secretary, in turn, asked Mr Pick, who was at that time the Institute's President, to ask the Railway Company to increase their contributions to make up for the Institute's lost revenues.

Without a usable Institute building the committee campaigned solidly to apply pressure on the executive of the North Eastern Railway Company, as owners of the building, to act. What may have been hurting the Shildon members by this point might have been that the company had erected new buildings for the other three principal Institutes in their region; York, Gateshead and Darlington. Shildon, the first of all railway institutes, perhaps felt it had been left behind.

At a prize-giving speech on Wednesday 8 Feb 1911, Alderman Jospeh Whitwell Pease was goaded by an attendee, Mr J D Rider, about the "beautiful Mechanics Institute" that had been long promised. It is highly probable that the North Eastern Railway had intended to open an Institute building at Shildon during 1911. It is also quite likely that it did not happen owing to a historic industrial dispute occurring that year.

1911 was the year in which the first National Railway Strike was called. It was the first railway related industrial dispute to involve rail workers from different companies right across Britain. The strike had been preceded by a series of localised disputes between railway workers and their employers, generally over pay and conditions. Industrial action on the North Eastern Railway had taken place during July 1910, triggered by events in Newcastle. This spat between workers and bosses flared up following the feeling of perceived injustice when a shunter was transferred to a new job for disciplinary reasons. Feeling incensed, signalmen, porters, drivers, guards and other grades of workers from Gateshead and the surrounding district did not show up for work on 19 July. This strike action spread throughout the North Eastern Railway area, with Shildon and Darlington railway workers quickly joining those withdrawing their labour in support of their colleague. The stand-off was ended when the company managers promised to investigate the grievances of workers. An undercurrent of discontent was still rife. A movement re-emerged within the union membership to resume a dormant campaign for an eight-hour working day for railwaymen. A separate movement among the same trade unionists sought to eliminate workers that would not become a member of a union, as they felt such men weakened their unified position. A withdrawal of labour was threatened unless the company desisted from employing non-unionised staff.

At the beginning of February 1911 tensions were further stoked by the dismissal of six North Eastern Railway company fish porters at Hull. The Shildon workers resolved to hold a vote on Sunday 5 February to decide whether to join the strike in support of their Hull branch colleagues. Strike action was averted when the company agreed that the case of the fish porters would be heard at the next meeting of the Conciliatory Board. A further local strike, centred on Shildon itself, was narrowly averted in May 1911. This particular tension had been stoked up after a closure of rail facilities at Tebay and Wear Valley Junction which had led to a number of the locomotive drivers and firemen from those sites being transferred to work at Shildon. After a number of the drivers had subsequently retired, being typically older than the firemen, it was found that there were too many firemen and, as not all the resulting driver vacancies had been filled, there was not enough work for the excess firemen. This strike was again averted, through the intervention and suggestions of George Tully, a driver and former chairman of Shildon Urban Council who suggested ways to run more trains staffed by the Shildon men.

In yet another example of these localised disputes in the build up to the national strike, an article in the Hartlepool Northern Daily Mail on Tuesday 11 July 1911 explained that the North Eastern Railway had been engaged in a dispute with the General Railway Workers Union, but had finally reached an agreement over improved pay for the various professions at rail works across the region. Additional money per-man would be gained for 'piece-work'. In terms of estimated equivalent value, the basic weekly wage of twenty-one shillings in 1911 would compare to earning just over ninety-eight pounds a week in 2020.

With a prevailing sentiment of discontentment simmering away, the railway workers unions were keen to provide a national demonstration of their unity and strength. They were particularly resentful of the formation of, and activities conducted by, the Conciliation Boards that had been set up to negotiate between railway workers and the companies. The railway companies, of course, preferred this approach to having to deal with the unions, as the outcomes were almost exclusively weighted in their favour. Unofficial industrial action across the workforce commenced during July and August of 1911. Eventually this triggered a convention of officials from the four principal rail unions at Liverpool, meeting with the purpose of co-ordinating national action. The outcome was that the unions jointly issued an ultimatum to the respective railway companies demanding that they accept direct negotiation with union representatives or face a national strike.

In a bid to avert this unprecedented strike, the Liberal Prime Minister, Herbert Asquith, advised rail companies that he would deploy police and troops to keep the trains running. Winston Churchill, the renowned Member of Parliament and future Prime Minister who had flip-flopped between Conservative and LIberal parties throughout is time in politics, was at this time a Liberal, and was the serving Home Secretary in Asquith's cabinet. Churchill moved to suspend the Army Regulation, which if left in place would have meant that the rail companies would themselves have had to request a military deployment for their protection. This change of regulation enabled the government to order troops to deploy to thirty-two towns across England and Wales. New Shildon was one of those places. Sensing this combined defiance of both government and rail companies as further provocation, the unions resolved to commit to their demonstration of national industrial action. The first Great National Rail Strike commenced over Friday 18 and Saturday 19 August 1911.

Here in Shildon, the latter of these two dates had long been scheduled to be the day of the annual Shildon Show. That event was of course severely disrupted by the consequent inability of visitors and exhibitors alike to reach the town by rail.

On the evening of 18 August, railway workers from Shildon and nearby Bishop Auckland held demonstrations. They marched through the streets, in time-honoured tradition, with union banners flying high and in columns headed by a brass band playing bold, uplifting and defiant march music. It was a powerful spectacle of working people making a stand for their rights.

A settlement to end this national strike action was achieved relatively quickly. But that national resolution did not, however, extend to resolving the underlying dispute between local employees and directors of the North Eastern Railway Company.

Railwaymen in the employ of other rail companies across

the rest of the nation returned victoriously to work, leaving only those employees in the principal North Eastern Railway towns and cities of Newcastle, South Shields, Tyne Dock, Gateshead, Darlington, York, Ferryhill, Hull, Shildon and Middlesbrough still on strike. Those men had commenced striking with other specific terms that were as yet unmet. Railwaymen across the region took new measures intended to be deliberately disruptive. Barricades were erected at the railway station in Leeds. In Darlington strikers burned straw and overturned a couple of railway trolleys before police intervened. At Shildon a signal box was attacked, with stones being thrown and breaking several of the window panes. Concerned by the prospect of more attacks, particularly on engineering like Shildon's Prince of Wales Tunnel, military units were relocated from York to both Darlington and Shildon.

This military presence was no small deputation. Fifteen-hundred hundred troops, from the Royal Inniskilling Fusiliers and East Yorkshire Regiments, arrived in Darlington on a heavy military train from York. Five-hundred of these were sent on to Shildon.

Far from having the effect of placating the combative railwaymen, this action further stoked their indignation. It had previously been reported in newspapers, so was well known among the men, that on 19 August 1911, at Llanelli railway station, two rail workers had been shot dead by troops from the Worcestershire Regiment. Nobody in Shildon wanted to see a repeat of this, yet they also did not want to concede their position.

Photographs taken during those few days show crowded meetings of railway workers taking place on the road between the gates of the company's works and the Masons Arms public house. Others depict the soldiers occupying strategic positions at the railway station, bridges, and on rooftops, monitoring the whereabouts of the strikers and ready to signal action. By 22 August, the number of troops at Shildon had been scaled back to either 130, or 200 depending upon which of the different newspaper reports was more accurate. These soldiers took up positions guarding the signal box, station and approaches to the railway sidings.

There continued to be further disturbances. In one instance a crowd attempted to set away some trucks that were standing on a siding. They were quickly driven away by the soldiers. Another incident saw a mineral train, that had been set up to make a run to Teesside, overcome by a crowd of demonstrators who chased off the strike-breaking driver and fireman by throwing stones. Elsewhere a young miner was captured throwing bricks at the locomotive of the military train, only to be released after giving his name and address.

Various reports estimate the number of active Shildon strikers to have been between two and four thousand. By Wednesday 23 August, the North Eastern strike was declared to be over, but the town of Shildon was perceived widely, due to the aggressive conduct of its men, to have shamed itself. The Jarrow Express of Friday 25 August 1911 read:

> With the exception of Darlington and Shildon the North Eastern men have been a pattern to others. No unseemly conduct has placed a black mark against them. Throughout all the week they have acted in an honourable and gentlemanly manner.

Its highly probable that the delay in providing the new Institute building, as evidenced by the year 1911 featuring on the stone tablet above the main door, was deliberate retribution for behaviours exhibited by the Shildon men during the strike. The incident was a blow to relations between company and employees.

However the new Institute building was indeed eventually erected, and came to be opened, whether by coincidence or by design, in what would have been the organisation's eightieth anniversary year. Whether intended or not, that does at least feel somewhat appropriate.

The Northern Echo reported on its grand opening taking place on 8 February 1913, telling how, after the doors had formally been opened, the lecture hall within was immediately crowded with railway officials and members of the Shildon and other North Eastern Railway Institutes, as well as members of the public.

Vincent Raven, then the Chief Mechanical Engineer of the North Eastern Railway, opened proceedings inside the new building with an explanation of how, for some years, the wagon works at Shildon had been growing, and consequently the town too. Due to that, and the condition of the older Institute building, the North Eastern directors had been approached with regard to a new Institute, which had led to the present gathering.

The silver-gilt key to the building was then presented as a memento to Arthur Pease, son of the older Arthur Pease who had been the MP for Darlington, by Mr R W Wordsell, manager of the works. Pease then gave a speech observing how he was no stranger to New Shildon and, referring to the prior generations of Peases being depicted in the portraits hanging around the hall, explained out that there were five generations of his family present in the room. Arthur mentioned that if his father, grandfather and great-grandfather had not been in some way closely connected with Shildon those pictures would not have been hanging on the walls. He noted that though he was a director of the North Eastern Railway, there were a number of shareholders equivalent to two-thirds of the company's workforce, and a balance had to be maintained between the interest of both groups. He noted also that he believed this institute was the oldest on the former Stockton and Darlington Railway route and hoped the building would be a very great blessing to the town, and that there would be many pleasant social gatherings in it for many years to come.

In his own speech, Vincent Raven highlighted that he was more acquainted with the institutes in York, Gateshead and Darlington, and though some of those were larger, none were better arranged or more comfortable than the newly built Shildon Railway Institute.

That older, now vacated, Institute building on Station Street was not destined for demolition straight away. It was was bought and converted to become a cinema under the name The Essoldo, granting it more years of life. Eventually however, it became commercially unviable as a cinema and stood derelict before its eventual demolition. Today nothing stands in that historic small square corner plot but trees shrubs and benches. A quiet place for rest and contemplation between the rows of houses.

Above: The new Railway Institute building erected by the North Eastern Railway which was opened to members in February 1913.

The new Institute building had been designed by the North Eastern Railway Company's Chief Architect, William Bell, of York, who had designed other railway buildings on the Shildon Works site, including the vast triple roundhouse locomotive shed that still stands on the site today. After the Beeching cuts of the sixties that building became a wagon repair workshop. Bell's new Institute has a three storey main block at the eastern end, with a single storey hall extending to the west. It is influenced by the Baroque Revival architectural style that Bell appears to have favoured at that time.

When you compare it with the NER's flagship offices at Stooperdale in Darlington, which were built in 1911, you can see that many of the architectural features are of identical style to the Institute. The common use of flying keystones over the windows and the festoon decorated apron beneath the central upper window of the main block, are both reminiscent of Baroque Revival. Likewise the use of pediments over the main entrance, dormers to allow light into the rooms accommodated beneath the roof space and the cornices are common to both buildings. Even the window frames on both buildings are almost exactly the same.

Above: The main hall of the new Redworth Road building when it opened in 1913. The platform at the front was where the speeches were given on opening day. Note the portrait collection around the walls.

The Stooperdale offices in Darlington, from where the NER's Chief Mechanical Engineer, Vincent Raven, designed so many of his remarkable locomotives, were clearly intended to be considered impressive. I think, therefore, that we ought to interpret it as a significant compliment to Shildon that both William Bell, and the North Eastern Railway Company deemed that its Institute building should be fashioned in similar style. Furthermore, looking at the other NER Institute buildings, in York, Gateshead and Darlington, you see that though they are situated in larger, more commercially important, places their design is more workmanlike and less ornate.

The building work to construct this new Institute building was contracted out to a Darlington builder named Albert Henry Earnshaw, a Stockton born man who at that time resided at East Mount Terrace in Darlington.

The main hall on opening day had a seating capacity for four hundred and eighty-six people. The ground floor hosted the Institute's library collection which at that time consisted of four thousand five hundred books. There was also a reading room and a magazine room which doubled as a ladies reading room. On the first floor there was a games room, a billiard room with four tables and a meeting room for the committee. Additionally there was a bathing room with three slipper baths for the use of members. The building was adorned throughout with engravings, prints, photographs, portraits and relics of the early days of steam. A second floor built into the roof space concealed spacious accommodation for a resident caretaker.

Having moved in to the new premises, the Institute committee set about revising the rules of the Institute to bring them up to date and reflect the new facilities it had to offer. The number of committee roles was expanded to become fifteen, still with an additional President but now with four Vice-Presidents instead of two. A further rule change was that in order to be eligible to put themselves forward to serve on the committee, candidates must be directly employed by the railway company. This was a criterion that had not been necessary in the past. Membership was not limited to railway employees; there were members, for example, that were teachers, shopkeepers and coal miners.

Once again, not everything about this new building was entirely perfect. The Institute's centenary book tells us that in 1914 a serious defect was revealed in the floor of the billiard room. It was necessary to close both that room, and the reading room beneath, for two months to allow re-laying of the floor.

The Institute worked quickly to put building's new main lecture hall to purposeful work. On 25 February, barely two weeks after the opening of the new building, a first lecture was given to members by Mr Ralph Hall Emmerson. The title was "My visit to Leasowe Castle Convalescent Home, and what I saw there."

In the days before Britain had a Welfare State many workers relied upon a range of charitable schemes, insurances and company backed institutions. The Railway Convalescent Homes was one such charitable organisation, having been founded in 1899 specifically to provide railway employees with one or two weeks free accommodation to recuperate from a serious illness, operation or to recover after an accident. That organisation built or acquired several properties around the country, of which Leasowe Castle on the Cheshire coast was but one.

Above: The reading room in the new Redworth Road building, as it was on opening day in February 1913. This space is now the members bar.

Ralph Emmerson had been born in 1864, lived on nearby Scott Street, and was employed at Shildon Works as a blacksmith. Quite how he came to spend time at Leasowe Castle is obscure, but we do know that he spoke of the benefits to be derived from a stay at one of the convalescent homes, of the care and consideration shown to visitors and the good fellowship he encountered there. His talk was illustrated by projected photographic slides so that those in his audience could see some

106

of the sights and facilities he highlighted throughout his speech. It's probable that Emmerson had been asked to speak on the subject rather than being the originator of the lecture, as the North Eastern Railway Magazine of April 1913 tells us that the lecture had been promoted by the Railway Convalescent Homes Committee, who were probably hopeful that Shildon's railway workers could be encouraged to subscribe, or donate, to the scheme.

It's also quite likely that Mr Emmerson had been in attendance at Leasowe Castle as a consequence of his own health. He would have been around 49 years old at the time of the lecture, and we do know that he passed away only four years later in 1917.

Ralph had at least three daughters and one son, who was also named Ralph Hall Emerson. This younger Ralph is worthy of mention here as he is one of the 250 persons named on the Institute's 1914-18 War Memorial which we'll take a look at in the next chapter. He was a wagon-builder who served in France in the Royal Engineers Railway Operating Division during that conflict. He returned home to Shildon afterward to resume his job at the railway works. Furthermore, the former soldier was not only a Methodist preacher who toured the North-East circuit, but also for some time President of the South Durham Adult School Union who had a school at Shildon. He also later fulfilled a charitable role in the community, that being president of the Shildon Branch of the Braille Guild.

In December 1913, Institute Committee member, Francis Bainbridge wrote a piece for the North Eastern Railway Magazine about the letter we mentioned in a previous chapter that had been written to Timothy Hackworth by George Stephenson and which was still then in the possession of the Committee at the Institute. As well as relating the content of the letter, Bainbridge spoke of the 'Dandy Cart' Stephenson had described. It was a vehicle used to convey the horses, that usually pulled the coal chaldrons along level sections of track, when trains of coal wagons were being hauled by rope up and down the inclines. Bainbridge wrote that there was a surviving example at Hackworth's old Soho Works buildings which, along with the letter and other artefacts, should be placed in a museum. He suggested that this museum should be built adjoining the Institute. Of course we know that nobody saw fit to progress the idea, which in hindsight could have been a marvellous one. It was perhaps ahead of its time given that it was almost a further century before the superb Locomotion railway museum was built at Shildon.

Into Conflict

The Institute, along with the rest of the world, was shaken considerably during 1914 by the outbreak of a World War, which would carry on until November of 1918. Much has been written elsewhere about this, and it is not our purpose here to tell that particular story. However, as everyone now knows, it was a catastrophic global conflict that touched the lives of so many families. Those of Shildon, and its surrounding towns and villages, were no different in this respect.

At the outset of this war, it was hoped that the conflict would be a brief affair, but even then it was clear that it would be important to rapidly expand the military forces of Britain, its Empire and its allies.

Over the four years during which war raged, men were drawn into the armed forces from all walks of life. Initially on a voluntary basis, and then increasingly through coercion, social pressure and eventually conscription. Women too were required to support the military forces in a variety of roles.

Initially the men working in the railway industries were designated as being necessary to their running, and hence made a protected occupation. Britain needed its engineering and logistics workers to keep the country functional, as well as to fuel the war with men and equipment. Railway engineers built special train carriages, to transport troops and treat battle casualties, as well as huge wagons to carry vehicles, heavy guns and ammunition.

As the war carried on, drawing in more of the nation's young men, schemes evolved to release young railwaymen from their employment, allowing them to volunteer for army and navy duties. Railway engineers, like miners, with their strength and engineering expertise, were particularly useful to the armed forces. Many, though not all, were drafted into Pioneer Battalions, the workhorse units of the army, or into railway operating divisions. They found themselves employed in a variety of engineering capacities; building tactical railway routes to the front, repairing, building roads, building and digging defences. Those that remained took on extra work creating weaponry and equipment for the frontline.

Throughout the entirety of the war a significant number of Shildon's men enlisted, some with permission of their employer, others without. Many of them did so at the recruiting office in nearby Bishop Auckland, though others travelled further afield to Newcastle or Sunderland. Some of them did not have to leave Shildon to enlist, signing up at special recruiting tour events. Of those Shildon recruits, a significant number were members of the Railway Institute.

Much has been written about so called 'pals battalions' where many groups of young men who worked together could join and serve together. The North Eastern Railway Company had raised one such battalion, the 17th Battalion Northumberland Fusiliers. However, our research has found that the young men and women of the Institute, for whatever reason, chose to enlist into a variety of different army units based at various locations around the country.

The committee of the Railway Institute moved quickly to recognise young men of that organisation that had signed up to serve their country. It was decided that all members who had joined the forces were to retain their membership, without payment of subscription, for the duration of their service. Additionally, where they had dependents, those dependents were permitted to use the Institute without charge for the duration of the war. This benefit was also bestowed upon soldiers in uniform.

As part of the home effort, the Shildon War Relief Committee and the NER War Savings Association were granted use of rooms of the Institute, and the Institute's cellar beneath the building was designated to serve as an air raid shelter should the enemy submit New Shildon to air attacks. This was a legitimate concern. It was an era during which communities lived in fear of visits from the dreaded Zeppelin airships which were seeking out industrial facilities such as those at New Shildon.

Updates on the activities of the Shildon Institute Branch of the War Savings Association's contributions were published in the North Eastern Railway's company magazine throughout the war. We know that the branch had 182 members, making it one of the largest branches in the association. Members bought coupons of stamps costing sixpence each, and for every 31 coupons of stamps they were awarded a certificate. In 1917 the War Savings Committee in London wrote a letter of appreciation to the North Eastern Railway Company to thank the railwaymen for their contributions.

As elsewhere across the British Empire, the war took its toll. Two hundred and fifty Institute members served during that so called 'Great War'. Four were female military or Red Cross nurses. Many of the former students of the Ambulance Association, which had been holding its classes in the main hall, joined the Royal Army Medical Corps. From the two hundred and fifty who served, a total of thirty men paid the ultimate price, losing their lives for their country's freedom. The Committee of the Institute were determined that this sacrifice should be remembered, and rather than simply remember the fallen, a memorial was commissioned to remember all of those that had also served.

This memorial, an arrangement of three plaques, was funded through family and member subscriptions, and was ordered from a company called Jones and Willis, who specialised in producing such memorials. It was installed and subsequently unveiled and dedicated on 8 November 1921 ahead of that year's Remembrance ceremonies. Major John Henry Smeddle and Archdeacon Derry were the principal guests of honour present at the unveiling.

Not all of the men listed on the memorial were from Shildon Works, there were others that were from the significant Railway Operating department at Shildon; engine cleaners, signalmen, lengthmen, shunters, drivers and firemen. It's important to remember too that the membership of the Institute also included men from other occupational backgrounds; teachers, shopkeepers, miners and clerks.

Presiding over the unveiling ceremony, Works Manager and Institute President, Robert William Worsdell expressed that the memory of those thirty men who had lost their lives could not be too highly esteemed or held to be too sacred. He hoped that all who looked upon their memorial would contemplate it with feelings of honour and respect for those who had passed.

Major Smeddle of the 8th Durham Light Infantry, son of New Shildon's Doctor Robert Smeddle and a resident of Darlington, had after the war returned to become a Running Superintendent of the NER's Railway Operating Division. He gave a speech to those assembled in which he said that he believed the men whose names had been inscribed on the memorial deserved the thanks of not only Shildon people, but of the whole British Empire. He commented upon how, in that post war era, the country had fallen upon very hard times and that it was necessary to endeavour to create the same spirit that had won the war so that problems, though difficult, would be solved.

An additional address was given by the Reverend T C Hillard, in the presence of Reverend Picton W Francis of All Saints Church and Reverend S F Warth.

After the assembly had sung the hymn "O God Our Help in Ages Past," the Shildon Male Voice Choir, under the baton of Henry Gibbon who had himself served in the 6th Durham Light Infantry, sang "Comrades in Arms," "The Souls of the Righteous," "The Reveille" and "Land of Hope and Glory". There can be no doubt that this moment would have evoked great and deep sentiment, especially among family members present.

The memorial is constructed of brass plaques on a wooden

mount. The centre plaque has a dome at centre top with the crest of the North Eastern Railway enamelled in patriotic colours. There is an engraved border of intertwined leaves set into an enamelled black background. Beneath it is the dedication, with the names of those who fell in battle engraved in two columns below. The two outer panels are headed in a red scroll "The following also" and "served with the colours". The other names are listed in four columns, with all lettering in Roman capitals.

The dedication on the memorial reads:

SHILDON NORTH EASTERN RAILWAY INSTITUTE, ROLL OF HONOUR, EUROPEAN WAR 1914-1918. TO OUR GLORIOUS DEAD. THE FOLLOWING MEMBERS GAVE THEIR LIVES FOR THEIR KING AND COUNTRY.

There are 250 names in total on the memorial - though only 30 are the names of men who did not return from the conflict. These are:

Name	Regt	Died
Pte. Thomas Alderson	20th DLI	31/07/17
Pte. Joseph H Atkinson	8th DLI	25/04/15
Pte. William Bamlett	20th DLI	21/09/17
Sgt. Harry Bundy	Royal Garrison Artillery	31/12/16
Pte. George Crawford	Kings Liverpool Rgt.	31/07/17
Pte. Sydney Doran	6th K. O. S. Borderers	26/04/18
Pte. Thomas E Emmerson	4th Kings Liverpool Rgt.	19/09/18
Pte. William Ewbank	18th DLI	22/06/16
Sgt. Thomas S Fletcher	6th DLI	01/10/16
Rfl. Alfred Graham	8th Kings R. Rifle Corps	15/09/16
Pte. Arthur Hardy	10th Lincs. Regiment	28/04/17
Cpl. Henry R Greener	Green Howards	07/10/17
Pte. Harold Harwood	Hampshire Rgt.	23/01/16
Pte. Fred Hall	2nd N'land Field Amb.	26/04/15
Pte. Herbert Trussler	12th Kings Liverpool Rgt.	04/10/18
AB George H Sykes	RN Reserve "Anson" Btn.	
L/Cpl. Thomas Ingledew	Coldstream Guards	09/10/17
Pte. George H Liddle	22nd DLI	04/03/17
Pte. William Ramage	7th Kings Liverpool Rgt.	27/09/18
Gnr. Samuel L Reeve	Royal Field Artillery	27/09/18
Pte. Albert E Robson	19th Kings Liverpool Rgt.	22/03/18
Pte. Thomas E Sayers	15th DLI	05/10/17
Pte. Thomas E Shafto	11th DLI	25/04/18
Pte. Harry Spensley	17th N'land Fusiliers	05/10/16

L/Cpl. Harry N Stanwix	Notts & Derbys Rgt.	21/03/18
Pte. Harry Stephenson	8th Yorks & Lancs Rgt.	29/10/18
Pte. John W Young	15th DLI	31/03/18
Pte. John Peacock	Machine Gun Corps	17/05/17
L/Cpl. George D Howe	6th DLI	05/11/16
Pte. Arthur Bowser	21st DLI	05/08/16

In 2021, to commemorate one hundred years since the unveiling of the Institute's war memorial, volunteers of the Shildon Heritage Alliance CIC, working in partnership with the Institute, invested many hours in research uncovering the individual stories of these men, and the others that served and returned, some bearing wounds. The resulting research document was published that year on the Institute's website. It relates the moving stories of the soldiers, sailors and airmen, as well as four nurses, with details of their family backgrounds, how they were employed, and where applicable the tragic stories and circumstances of their deaths.

Above: The war memorial installed in 1921 to remember Institute members who fell, or who served, in the First World War

From that Remembrance weekend in 2021 onward, a

tradition of placing poppy wreaths on the stairwell has bene resumed. It is done on the Saturday before Remembrance Sunday, in tribute to the sacrifice of Institute members in that conflict.

Not all of the survivors returned to Shildon to resume their jobs in the town. For a variety of reasons, some demobilised soldiers chose to move on and to establish a new life elsewhere.

There was another tragic wartime death with a connection that touched New Shildon and the Institute. This occurred closer to home, and during the last year of the First World War.

The incident took place on Tuesday 12 February 1918. A pilot, Second-Lieutenant A H Birkbeck had become lost in fog and was attempting to return to his aerodrome. He had descended almost to ground level to attempt to get his bearings from landmarks on the ground, but had afterwards been unable to get his engine to pick up again sufficiently to lift the aeroplane over a hedge ahead of him as he was running along the surface of a farmer's field.

Unfortunately for all concerned, two children were nearby and hearing the noise from the plane had nipped through a gap in the hedge to try to catch sight of it. The pilot later claimed that he had not seen the children as he accidentally knocked down and killed eleven-year-old Edith Walker of Thomas Street, only a short distance from the Institute.

The Institute, as we have already explained, was regularly requisitioned to be used for coroner's inquests, and this occasion was no different. The inquest was held the next day and the coroner returned a verdict of accidental death, exonerating the young pilot.

In December 1921, some months after the War Memorial had been installed in the Institute, there was a further interesting incident that is reported in the Institute's Centenary Book of 1933. A fire had broken out inside the Institute. Something had ignited in the upstairs Committee Room. It's worth remembering that even though in those days the Institute had a central heating system with radiators, there were still several open fireplaces, and coal was a plentiful and cheap source of heating. It was also a time when doubtless smoking of pipes, cigarettes and cigars would have been commonplace around the building.

The fire was quickly spotted and dealt with effectively before much damage could be done to building and furniture. This is fortunate as the effects could otherwise have been devastating.

Marking the First Hundred Years

In 1933, the Shildon Railway Institute reached its hundredth year, and by then yet another railway company had become its patron.

After the First World War the Railways Act of 1921 was passed, and consequently, on 1 January 1923 railway companies across Britain were merged into one of what were referred to as the 'Big Four' railway companies. The whole operating and engineering estate of the North Eastern Railway became part of the London and North Eastern Railway, or LNER.

The Institute was in good health at that time having a reported membership of 732 persons. The LNER were determined to play a part in marking the hundredth year of the world's first Railway Institute. A Centenary Committee was formed, and plans were drafted for a grand exhibition of modern locomotives and rolling stock at the Shildon Works.

In advance of the celebrations, Francis Bainbridge researched and wrote a Centenary Book chronicling the Institute's first hundred years. This was published and circulated by the committee, with promotional snippets being printed in several newspapers nationwide in the build up to the much anticipated event. Copies were sold to exhibition visitors and Institute members for sixpence.

The celebratory proceedings commenced on Sunday 24 September 1833, with a formal opening by William Whitelaw, chairman of the LNER. Sir Murrough J Wilson presided over the whole event, aided by other LNER directors; Major W Henton Carver MP and Clarence D Smith. Also in attendance were the LNER's renowned Chief Mechanical Engineer, Herbert Nigel Gresley, and his Assistant Chief Engineer, Arthur Cowie Stamer.

Whitelaw began by visiting the Institute building on Redworth Road to watch Stamer unveil a special celebratory bronze tablet in the building. He then proceeded to the works to open the exhibition at half past ten in the morning. In introducing Mr Whitelaw, the President stated:

> "Mr Whitelaw needs no introduction to any body of railwaymen, and no one entertains a greater affection for his brother railwayman than does our chairman. He has very much at heart the ideal of keeping going that spirit of comradeship which we used to have on the old NER, which we used to find on the North British line, and which we hope to maintain in our present great

organisation."

Mr Whitelaw, himself responded:

"It was not very easy 100 years ago to start such projects, because people were not then giving much thought to institutes or to the aim of providing means of educational and moral improvement for those who worked for them. These pioneers of 100 years ago realised the necessity of giving men more to do than merely building or repairing rolling stock. They saw the need of an Institute where intellectual and social progress could be made after a day's work was done. They realised that only along these lines could real progress be made."

Above: The centenary commemoration plaque unveiled by A C Stamer on 26 September 1933.

He went on to talk of the severe economic troubles that were affecting everyone in the early nineteen-thirties, and expressed a belief that Shildon would become known as one of the greatest places on the railway system if every man does his part in helping his neighbour to get over his worst trouble.

Interestingly, not everyone was satisfied with the arrangements for the Institute's centenary celebration. The Newcastle Evening Chronicle of 12 September 1933 explained that the clergy and ministers of Shildon sent a letter to the Shildon LNER Institute Centenary Committee expressing their regrets about the event. The signatories advised that they shared the giving of thanks for one-hundred years of the Institute, but pointed out that the opening was happening at the same time as church services were being held, so they had been unable to identify themselves with the rejoicing. They were also disappointed at not having been invited to participate in planning the arrangements.

Nonetheless, the exhibition was a tantalising opportunity for rail enthusiasts. To the stirring sounds of musical selections played by the LNER Shildon Silver Band, its visitors were treated to a majestic display of twelve locomotives and fourteen items of rolling stock. The exhibits present were itemised in a programme created for the occasion.

Above: Nigel Gresley's high-pressure compound express locomotive No. 10000 was a centrepiece at the LNER's 1933 Shildon exhibition to commemorate the centenary of Shildon Railway Institute.

Gresley's Engine No. 10000.

With conceptual development commencing in 1924 and completing in 1929, this was something of a rock-star exhibit. Locomotive 10000 never bore a name, but was often referred to as the "Hush-Hush" on account of the secrecy surrounding it. It was a 4-6-4 four-cylinder tender locomotive with a unique streamlined appearance.

An entirely different locomotive to others running at the time, it was fitted with a Yarrow-Gresley water tube boiler instead of the usual smoke tube type. Though it was not to be a successful locomotive it was distinctively styled and eye catching enough in looks to have served as the iconic graphic used on the cover illustration for the Institute's centenary book and event programme.

Class A1 Pacific.
A three-cylinder 4-6-2 super heated passenger express locomotive that was used for the east coast express routes. These Gresley designed locomotive types were built from 1922, with the last ones being withdrawn from service in 1948.

Class D 49 "Shire"
Three-cylinder locomotives with a 4-4-0 wheel configuration that had first been pioneered in the USA, becoming popular here later for its economy. This again was a super heated passenger engine. Built yet again to Gresley's designs the D49 class was first built in 1927 and continued in service until 1961. They earned the class name "Shire" on account of individual locomotives being named after shire counties.

Electric Locomotive No. 13
It is often forgotten that as well as being a pioneering steam locomotive town, Shildon was a pioneering electric railway town. At the beginning of the 1910s the former route of the old Clarence Railway to Newport, north of the mouth of the Tees, was electrified, and the North Eastern Railway, who had first experimented with electric locomotives on Tyneside, set up a full scale experiment hauling coal using a fleet of ten bo-bo electric locomotives, all of which were stabled at Shildon. These were numbered 2 to 12, and were designed by Sir Vincent Raven. They were hugely successful. This thirteenth locomotive was an advanced design with main line electrification in mind, and was built at Darlington. The project was discontinued owing to changes in demand for coal transport. But it's worth noting that the east coast main line was eventually electrified, proving that Raven and the NER were right in principle.

Class K 3 "Mogul"
A three-cylindered 2-6-0 locomotive that was used at that time for heavy main line freight trains. These superseded earlier 0-6-0 designs that had been preferred for freight haulage. They were again the work of Gresley and first built in 1921. The last left service in 1961.

Class J 39

These were two-cylinder 0-6-0 engines built for heavy fast goods trains. Their predecessors had been locomotives designed around 1874 by William Bouch at Shildon for the Stockton & Darlington Railway, but there had been several iterations of the J class updated by designers like Stirling and Worsdell, Drummond, Reid and Holmes. Gresley's 1926 take on the J class, the J39, had larger wheels than its immediate predecessor and became the LNER's group standard 0-6-0 locomotive.

Class T 1

The T1 was a heavy hump shunting engine designed by Wilson Worsdell. It was a tank engine with a 4-8-0 wheel configuration ideal for moving coal wagons for loading onto ships. They were all eventually withdrawn from duties between 1955 and 1961.

Class X1 "Aerolite"

A two-cylinder 2-2-4 engine, and in 1933 one of the oldest passenger engines still in service, though at that time it was being used either for "Officers Specials" trips or inspecting the line. The original "Aerolite" was built in 1851 with a 2-2-2 configuration. It was replaced with No. 66 "Aerolite" in 1869, and much modified in subsequent years. The LNER used to keep "Aerolite" at Darlington where it was used by A C Stamer until his retirement during the same year as the Institute centenary celebrations. After that it was taken to York for preservation. More recently, and throughout the time of writing this book, Aerolite has returned to Shildon and was quite fittingly, though not deliberately, present in town for the Institute's 190th year, and is displayed at the Locomotion museum.

Class A 5

The A5 was another variant of the Pacific locomotives, this time with a side tank and water pick up gear. It was to a John G Robinson design. It had two cylinders and was used predominantly for heavy branch traffic and short distance excursion trains. It had a 4-6-2 wheel configuration. 44 of these locomotives were built in total.

Class Y 1

These were 0-4-0 Sentinel locomotives used mainly for light shunting duties, particularly where tight curves were involved in the track layout. They were so specialist that they were not created in large numbers. The Y 1 class was first built in 1927, with the last ones being withdrawn in 1958.

Above: The locomotive "Aerolite" was also part of the 1933 Shildon Railway Institute centenary exhibition, and recently returned to Shildon to be displayed at the Locomotion museum.

Class C 9

The LNER's C 9 was another Gresley design, being a rebuild of the C 7 class. They were 4-4-2 Atlantic 'booster' locomotives of the type that dominated the route between Aberdeen and Kings Cross. The C 9 variant was officially designated in February 1932 so would have been quite a new development at the time of the exhibition.

Diesel Electric Locomotive

A single car passenger locomotive fitted with a 250 brake horse power Armstrong Sulzer diesel engine. It had room for 60 passengers and was able to hit speeds of 65 miles per hour. These units, combining both locomotive and carriage in one single vehicle, were considered cutting-edge transport innovations in 1933 having only been introduced the previous year. In some respects they were the forerunners of the Pacer diesel railbuses that became a familiar sight from the nineteen-eighties onwards.

The rolling stock section of the exhibition included a Buffet Car, Pullman Car considered the last word in luxury travel, Triplet Restaurant Car Set, Third Class Sleeping Car, Mail Van, Holiday Camping Coach, 30 Ton Trestle Plate Wagon, 40 Ton Hoppered Coal Wagon, Chaldron Wagon, 50 Ton Sulphate Wagon, Alumina Ore Wagon, Container Wagon with 5 Ton Steel Container, Platelayer's Trolley and a Snow Plough Set.

There was also an accompanying model exhibition presenting models of locomotives, stationary engines, power houses, bridges and a sea-plane. Overall, the exhibition represented a grand day out, and was an impressive demonstration of the respect held by the LNER board for the Shildon Institute and its unique and fascinating place in the world's rail story.

Railway Queens and More Conflict

The latest Institute building, and particularly its main hall, continued to be a focal point for entertainments.

In December 1922, for example, the Shildon Orchestral Society, comprising predominantly of railway company employees, performed a programme of music conducted by William Grandy, consisting of Offenbach's "Orpheus in the Underworld", Bucolossi's "Monsieur Beaucaire," Thurbarr's "Americana," and Charles Ancliffe's military waltz "For Valour". There were additional vocal items by Di Duca and Charles Larman. The large audience in attendance reportedly commented on the orchestra's improvement.

Occasionally the entertainments at the Institute were more competitive in nature, involving several bands to provide a full programme to enjoy. In one such example, a dance band contest held in February 1932, three dance bands from across the region gave their best in competition for a cash prize and a handsome silver cup. The Plaza Dance Orchestra of West Hartlepool beat their home town rivals, the Mayfair Orchestra, as well as the New Corona Band from Spennymoor, who appear to have been quite regularly engaged at Institute entertainments.

Another occasional visitor to the Institute was Britain's Railway Queen, the winner of a contest that was held annually, except during the Second World War when it was suspended. The contest was initiated in 1925 as part of the celebrations to mark the centenary of the opening of the Stockton and Darlington Railway, and became one of the means by which relations were maintained between railway company managers, workers and the trade unions.

Candidates for the title of Railway Queen were originally selected from girls aged between 12 and 16 from railway workers' families. Hundreds of girls entered each year and these were narrowed down to a final shortlist representing each area.

The final took place at a carnival at Belle Vue, Manchester, which became one of the biggest social gatherings of rail workers on the annual calendar. The winner would be crowned with a tiara, and adorned with both a chain of office and a royal blue embroidered jewel encrusted gown.

On being declared Railway Queen, their duty thereafter would be to travel the country, visiting offices and works, to boost morale among the workforce and promote charitable purposes that benefitted railway workers. These included railway housing schemes, convalescent homes and, particularly, in those years before the founding of a National Health Service, hospitals run as charitable endeavours. It was a significant workload and responsibility for so young a person. The Railway Queen would also act as an ambassador in an international capacity, having opportunity to visit a country in Europe, or perhaps the USA or Russia, taking messages from British railway workers. From these visits a tradition grew, which was that when the Railway Queen visited another country she would receive an additional link for her chain of office as a gift from the railway workers there.

On a busy tour of duty, in May 1936, the Railway Queen that year, Audrey Mossom of Blackpool who had been crowned in 1935, visited Shildon. She was promoting the Railwaymen's Cottage Homes and Orphans Funds as well as the Bishop Auckland Cottage Hospital fund, which was patronised by Sybil Lady Eden. Miss Mossom visited Bishop Auckland first, where she was greeted at the station and joined a procession, headed by the Shildon Wesleyan Band, en route to the Bishop's Park for a formal civic reception. Later she led-off a dance at Bishop Auckland's LNER Institute before attending a function at the Shildon Railway Institute. It was the following year, however that was perhaps the most exciting for Shildon.

In 1937, the lass crowned as twelfth Railway Queen at Belle Vue was none other than Miss Irene Topham, aged 15, of King Edward Street, Shildon. Her throne at the grand crowning ceremony in Manchester was a chair that was said to have been used by George Stephenson during his work on the construction of the Liverpool to Manchester Railway.

Prior to attaining the title of Queen, Irene, despite her youth, worked in a bakers and confectionery shop. Her father Thomas was a signalman, and her brother worked at the Shildon Works. The family lived at 22 Raby Gardens. She was the only Railway

Queen to have come from our town. It was estimated by the press that between forty and sixty-thousand members of the nation's railway employees and their dependents attended the carnival at which she was crowned. Special trains had been arranged from ninety places across England and Wales.

A special service of dedication for her was held on the evening of Sunday 17 October at the Methodist Church on Shildon's Soho Street. The Newcastle Journal reported that Irene had announced the hymns and read the scripture lesson, while the Rev W J Penberty-White commented on the uniqueness of the occasion remarking that none of her predecessors had commenced their year of office with the benediction of the church.

Later that year, it was announced that Irene's international destination was going to be Sweden. This brief Scandinavian trip took place in May 1938, and Irene was tasked with a special additional duty of conveying a message from Shildon Railway Institute. Prior to departure, she was handed a laurel wreath, by Mr W Wells-Hood, the General Manager of the LNER Shildon Works, to place at the statue of pioneering Swedish railway engineer John Ericsson which stood in the city of Gothenburg. The card attached to the wreath conveyed the following message:

"A token of regard to the genius of John Ericsson from the members of the Shildon Railway Institute, the oldest railway institute in the world."

The connection, prompting and inspiring the Committee of the Institute to send this gift, was that Ericsson had been the locomotive engineer behind the engine "Novelty," which had competed at the Rainhill Trials at Liverpool in 1829, alongside Stephenson's locomotive "Rocket" and our own Timothy Hackworth's "Sans Pareil". In a try-out before the day of the contest Ericsson's locomotive broke down, and Timothy Hackworth, who as we know later became the Institute's first President, attempted to assist him.

Irene's tour in Sweden took her as far as the power station at Porjus in the arctic circle. She told a reporter that she was excited to see the reindeer and meet the Lapps.

Irene's year as the Rail Queen ended on Monday 31 August 1938 whereupon a special concert was organised at the Institute by the Shildon Branch of the NUR Women's Guild on behalf of the Orphan Fund. This final act of charity was her last official public engagement as Queen. She was presented with gifts of a reading lamp and a case of tea knives. In return, Mr Clarkson, on behalf of the Institute committee, received a framed photograph of the retiring Queen.

Above: Irene Topham, the only British Railway Queen to have come from Shildon, meets railway porters at Manchester's Victoria Station in 1937. This was the day before she was crowned. In the following year she took a special message from the Institute to Sweden.

Though Irene was the only National Railway Queen to originate from Shildon, many of the others visited Shildon, and its Institute, on their own tours. For example, in 1950 Shildon held a small event to mark the centenary of the passing of Timothy Hackworth. A special committee was convened, specifically to plan how to commemorate the date, and a special souvenir booklet was produced to explain the historic significance of Hackworth and his technological achievements, along with details of what would happen at the ceremony. To make the event particularly special, the committee had invited the newly elected British Railway Queen, Miss Janet Evelyn Hubbard of Ely in Cambridgeshire, to visit Shildon and play a key part in the ceremony. Her visit here was scheduled to take place straight after her international ambassadorial visit to Norway.

The ceremony began at 6:45pm on Friday 7 July 1950, exactly 100 years to the day after Hackworth had passed away. Janet's part was to lay a wreath at Hackworth's grave in St John's Churchyard, before a united service was held near Hackworth's statue in the park. Music was provided by the town's British Railways Band accompanying a combined choir. The following day a special celebratory social evening was held at the Institute.

Ms Hubbard, who married Peter Handley in 1954 to become Mrs Handley, retained memories of her visit to Shildon and her time as Railway Queen, and in July 2013, she wrote a letter to Shildon Railway Institute, enclosing her copy of the souvenir booklet. It had been signed for her by each of the twenty members of the Hackworth event committee, as well as the Clerk of the Council. She wrote:

"I had a wonderful year as Railway Queen - tea on the terrace in the Houses of Parliament, two weeks escorted holiday in Norway etc. I don't know whether it is still held nowadays, I haven't heard anything. I am now 80 but the memories are still very clear."

The signed booklet now forms part of the Institute's revived library and archive collection, which we'll come to later. A few years later in 1957 we were visited by Teresa Boyden of Peterborough as part of her tour. In 1973 the serving queen for that year visited the Institute to attend the Farewell Party for the retiring Production manager, Mr Hume. It's worth reflecting that the Railway Queen contests served as inspiration for other British industries to make similar arrangements leading to the emergence of such as the Cotton Queen, Potteries Queen, Tobacco Queen and Coal Queen contests.

Another regular attraction at the new Institute was the Shildon LNER Works Band. Like many towns across both region and nation, Shildon had a strong tradition of brass band and ensemble music. The first successful band associated with the New Shildon area was the New Shildon Saxhorn Band, founded by rail worker Francis Dinsdale and his sons Edward and Anthony. That band is often mentioned in Institute report books as having performed at the older Institute building, and it is recorded in membership books that Francis was a member.

Above: Janet Hubbard, Britain's Railway Queen in 1950, visited Shildon and the Railway Institute as part of commemorations of the centenary of Timothy Hackworth's death.

Dinsdale's grandson, Thomas Bulch, became a talented and ambitious musician in his own right. Bulch, whose father was the locomotive fireman that we previously told of being almost killed in a derailment on the South Durham and Lancashire Union line, became bandmaster of the breakaway New Shildon Temperance Band and was also a member of the Institute. Thomas became a published brass band composer before leaving Shildon in 1884, with three of his bandmates, to enjoy a distinguished career as a professional bandmaster, composer, conductor, publisher and band contest judge in Victoria, Australia. He is perhaps best known, though not entirely well known, for unknowingly playing a part in the story of how the unofficial Australian anthem "Waltzing Matilda" came to sound as it does. It would be misleading to say that he composed the music for it. Bulch was a violinist as well as a cornet player, and while in Australia, arranged a march based upon a traditional folk song by Robert Tannahill and James Barr that had been included in a violin medley by a Glaswegian, Archibald Milligan, who created music under a pseudonym, Carl Volti. Bulch also used a pseudonym, Godfrey Parker, to publish that march, which was entitled "Craigielee." That march was heard by Christina MacPherson at Warnambool Races, who in turn played it from memory to Banjo Patterson, who used it as the tune to his new Australian folk song. It is a complicated chain of events, but Bulch's role is clear. Back home, the New Shildon Temperance Band, which he played a part in founding, lived on to become the LNER Works Brass Band.

Another Institute member who is greatly respected in the brass band fraternity, and is still revered today for his timeless and phenomenally good brass band contest marches, was George Allan. Both Allan and Bulch were apprenticed at the same time in the blacksmith's department at Shildon Works. Allan, however, later became a wagon painter. When Francis Dinsdale, his musical mentor, died he took control of the New Shildon Saxhorn Band, and supplemented his income by selling his own brass band compositions to publishers. Like Bulch, he too earned fees for judging band contests. In his later years he published sheet music himself from his little house at 2 Pears Terrace, a mere stone's throw from both the older Station Street and newer Redworth Road Institute buildings. George and his wife, Elizabeth, were members of the Institute at Shildon for much of their lives. Although he remained an amateur musician to the end, Allan is considered by the brass banding community to be one of the greats of his generation.

Both Allan and Bulch died in 1930, but their legacies lived on both here in Shildon, and more widely across the British Empire. Allan's marches "Knight Templar," "Raby" and "The Wizard" are among those still played widely today, still helping bands win prizes at band contests. Between the two composers, they created over four-hundred-and-fifty pieces of music, and their often surprising life story has been researched and told by the author of this book in another entitled "The Wizard and The Typhoon".

It was, therefore, a normal occurrence that the dominant brass band in Shildon would hold concerts at the Institute, and that some of the music heard at those concerts would have been created in Shildon by one of these two Institute members.

On Sunday 2 April 1939, for example, we are told that the LNER Band gave a concert at the Institute, under their regular conductor, Mr Collinson. The programme included songs from the contralto singer Miss Mary Noble, and Mr R Barnett, whose wife also accompanied on piano.

Above: The LNER Shildon Works Silver Band with bandmaster T W Collinson show off a selection of their trophies in this photograph taken inside the Institute.

The bandmaster was Shildon born Thomas William Collinson. He spent time as a gas fitter and plumber in the employment of the railway company. He had learned to play as a lad in the Shildon Silver Band before joining the army as a bandsman in the Sherwood Fusiliers during the First World War. His military career then took him to the 59th Divisional Band before being demobilised. He returned home to play with the Eldon Colliery Band before moving to direct the Rushden Temperance Band, which he guided to become Durham Association Champions in 1933. From there his career as a band master took him to Brandon, whom he left in February 1935. This was the moment when the, by now very experienced, Thomas felt ready to take charge of the LNER Shildon Works band, which later became the Shildon British Railways Band. He stayed in that post until 1951.

Under Collinson's leadership the LNER Shildon Works Silver Band experienced significant band contest success. This began with being placed first at the local Shildon band contest in June 1937. Perhaps their finest achievement was being placed first in the Durham County Band League Contest in July 1946. During his tenure the band was usually in the Second Section of the North of England Area Contests, so considered to be quite accomplished. His successor was Mr A Bagley who stayed with the band until 1975, a period during which the band competed in the less prestigious Fourth Section.

The end of the 1930s, of course, brought the outbreak of the Second World War, with the chaos, pain and frugality that accompanied it. During those years the Institute once again acted a hub for initiatives associated with war relief.

The New Shildon Womens' Institute for example closed December 1939 by holding a dance in the Institute's Main Hall with the objective being to raise money to buy wool with which to create comforts for the soldiers away on duty. The event was a success, bringing in an estimated 300 people. There were competitions with spot prizes, which were awarded by Captain Wakefield, and music was provided by Bob Murton's Dance Band.

The Institute of the early decades of the twentieth century also had associations with amateur boxing, with contests occasionally taking place there. An amateur boxing club of rail workers was formed in 1903, during the North Eastern Railway era, which continued through the LNER and British Rail eras, and happily is still a going concern in the present day.

For many years the club trained at what is now one of the few buildings remaining from Timothy Hackworth's Soho Works. It was a decent space for sparring, but not suitable for staging boxing matches with an audience. The opening of Shildon's 1913 Institute building, however, created an excellent venue for the public to watch their local boxers in action.

On 24 May 1939, for example, fights were hosted as part of the North Yorkshire and South Durham Junior Boxing League. One of the victors was J Trotter of Shildon who had been undefeated in the league, and on that occasion bested his opponent R Sanderson of the Joe Walton Club, Middlesborough.

The contests didn't always take place at the Institute, but when they didn't, prizes gained would still be presented there. In March 1939 LNER Boxing Championship cups were presented to E Jenkinson for winning the London Great Eastern Cup contest that season, the flyweight J Hall for his win in the York contest. Other prizes were handed to the bantamweight H Horner, welterweight E Jenkinson and middleweight S Cottingham.

This last boxer, Syd Cottingham, went on to be widely regarded as having been one of Shildon's greatest ever boxers. He was born on 9 February 1914, a year and a day after the new Institute building opened. By 1937 he had become LNER all-England middleweight champion and represented England internationally. That same year, aged 23, he fought and beat Bruce Woodcock on points at Doncaster. Bruce Woodcock went on to become British heavyweight champion. In 1939, the year that Syd won as a middleweight at the York contest, he was employed by the LNER as a machinist in the machine shop at Shildon Works and was living with his wife, Mary, and two children at 7 Plevna Street, Shildon. In 1948 he won the British Railways (North East Region) heavyweight championship at York.

Above: A young J Trotter (left) of Shildon takes on R Sanderson in a boys boxing bout held at the Institute in May 1939

Other boxing greats from the Shildon club over the years include Tommy Wearmouth, Eddie Jenkinson, John Walton, Charlie Raine, Bob Tully and Cecil Attwood.

In the late twentieth century, Shildon Amateur Boxing Club, often nomadic, changed its base of operations several times, and we shall return to them in a future chapter.

During the Second World War, the nation adopted an attitude of austerity. It didn't seem appropriate to celebrate while our fighting forces were experiencing hardship abroad, and the nation needed to save its money and resources to bolster the war effort. The organising committee of the annual Shildon Show agreed not to hold events while the war was underway. But there were occasional moments here and there designed to keep up the morale of Shildon folk, and the Institute played its part in bringing people together.

On Saturday 13 January 1940 for example, the committee of the Shildon Old People's Christmas Treat Fund held a "high tea' for about 400 of the town's oldest residents at the Institute.

The Institute also continued to be a focal point for fundraising events in connection with the war effort. A society was formed in the town to raise money for soldiers comforts which, despite being based at the town's Temperance Hall, would hold regular fundraising whist drives, and the occasional concert or dance, at the Institute.

The British Railways Era Begins

In 1947, following the end of the Second World War, the Government passed the Transport Act 1947, which made provision to nationalise the 'Big Four' railways companies and unite them under a single brand. This came into effect on the 1 January 1948, whereupon all assets of the London and North Eastern Railway, including the Institute building at Shildon, became the property of British Railways.

From the early months of 1948 onward there are numerous reports from around the country referring to new regional branches of an overarching British Railways Staff Association. This was the subsidiary organisation that absorbed all of the social facilities belonging to the former regional railways. Yet the British Railways Staff Association was not formally inaugurated nationally until 1 January 1952. Its upcoming formalisation was announced in advance in the pages of the November 1951 issue of the British Railways Magazine for staff.

All 600,000 railway staff across the country became eligible for membership, and the membership would encompass not only current serving, and retired, railwaymen, but also their wives or widows and dependent children.

The Institute at Shildon becoming part of this umbrella organisation, bound by its rules, also meant changing its own membership policy. We know from studying the occupations of members, such as those that served or died during the Great War, that during the North Eastern Railway era, that as in previous eras, membership had not been restricted exclusively to railwaymen and their families. Many of the local teachers were members of the Institute, as were some coal miners or people that ran the other shops and businesses that supported the rail industry in the town. Moving forward many of these folk would be excluded.

There was however an early stated intention to extend the opportunity of membership to staff of the other executive divisions of the British Transport Commission wherever that was deemed practical.

This restriction of membership and access to the Institute to employees of British Railways, or British Rail as it became after 1965, was written into the rules of the British Railways Staff Association Shildon Branch, which now superseded the Institute's own rules. They remained in place right through the remainder of the British Rail era and, through not having been reviewed by subsequent iterations of committee, continued to be the case for almost four decades after British Rail ceased employing workers in Shildon. It simply hadn't seemed important to change them even thought they hadn't been so strictly enforced from 1984 onward.

Throughout the BRSA tenure of the Institute, it wasn't enough that someone had worked for British Rail or its forerunners in the past. Members had to be current employees or, if not, they should have served at least two years in the service of the company. A classification of Associate Member was later introduced, for friends of qualifying railway workers, but the overall policy led to an ingrained popular perception throughout Shildon during those decades and beyond, that the Institute was only for the railwaymen and their families. During the town's later post-industrial era, that belief contributed to dwindling membership and a gradual decline in the Institute's fortunes.

It was only after a long overdue review of the membership rules in 2020 that they were at last officially changed to permit people to apply for membership regardless of whether or not they had ever been, or were a bona-fide family member of, a British Rail employee.

Back in 1952, British Railways were enthused at the prospect of the benefits of their newly inaugurated Staff Association. It was intended that it would offer, at small cost, the opportunity to participate in all kinds of sports, pastimes, music, drama, arts, crafts and other social recreational and cultural events. Aside from the reduced emphasis on access to educational facilities this announcement was very much in the spirit of what the Institute at Shildon had already become under its previous three railway company patrons, so represented a continuation.

An intention was announced to hold competitions within the association on a regional basis with branches taking each other on to foster a sense of belonging within the wider movement.

Membership of the BRSA, under its national terms, was to be voluntary and accessed for a weekly subscription of four pence per week per member. This was generally deducted directly from each worker's pay. The proceeds from the resulting fund would be used to finance local and regional activities, administration of the organisation as a whole, and to subsidise smaller branches. A further consequence was that the responsibility for the ongoing maintenance of facilities such as the Railway Institute at Shildon fell to the BRSA rather than British Railways as a whole. British Railways, in announcing its staff association, with all the benefits that brought, recognised that full regard had to be given to the provision of amenities for social and recreative purposes. On this front they had some specific plans in mind for Shildon.

A New Sports Ground

In the closing weeks of 1954, Shildon British Railways Cricket Club, were looking to make improvements to their game. The club had been founded in association with the Institute back in 1913, later becoming the town's LNER Cricket Club and thus was now part of the recently formed British Railways Staff Association. Their first step was to appoint a new professional player and coach, in the form of Jack Watson.

Watson had been a Northumberland County player with Washington and Alnwick, and had also topped the batting and bowling averages in that league during the previous season. The Shildon BR side were playing in the Durham County League having graduated from the Mid-Durham Senior League.

But perhaps the most significant and exciting step-up in the team's fortunes was the planned opening of a brand new BR Sports Ground the following spring. Up until that point the cricket team had used a field adjacent to the west end of the railway works. The new ground boasted not only a cricket pitch, but a host of other facilities including a bowling green, football pitch and a fine pavilion.

As with every major improvement the Institute members had worked to achieve throughout their history, the opening of the new Sports Ground was celebrated with a grand event, which was scheduled to take place on Saturday 14 May 1955. In keeping with the theme of the day the main focus was a sequence of different sporting contests and demonstrations. A simple four page souvenir programme was created and sold to interested parties for sixpence each.

The committee of the British Rail Staff Association Shildon Branch, which would now be responsible for two sites, was expanded to include the voices of representatives from each of the sporting sections; cricket, bowls, tennis, football at senior and junior level, gymnasium, athletics and physical culture. The latter we might refer to now as bodybuilding. So as to not be excluded from having a voice, additional representatives were added to speak on behalf of the British Railways Shildon Band and the dancers. There were also political sections represented, covering branch members from both the National Union of Railwaymen and the Amalgamated Engineering Union.

The much anticipated opening event for the new Sports Ground commenced at 2:30pm with two sporting matches taking place concurrently. On the virgin surface of the cricket pitch onlookers could watch the local cricketing heroes of Shildon BR take on Dawdon Colliery Welfare, in what was the first Durham County League fixture to take place there. On the new bowling green Shildon BR competed against a team from Brandon, near Durham.

These contests were followed at 3:45pm by the official ceremony in which the guest of honour, Mr H A Short CBE, General Manager of the British Rail North East Region gave a speech and formally opened the sports ground. At intervals selections of music were performed by the British Rail Shildon Band.

Later in the afternoon, from 5:30pm onwards, a Grand Boxing Tournament took place consisting of five contests each of three rounds of two-minute duration. These were officiated over by E F Jenkinson Esquire, with P Thomas, C Richardson and S Cottingham adjudicating.

The final sporting event of the day was an exhibition of weight lifting organised by the "physical culture" section, in which R Raine and D Holmes took turns in attempts to outdo each other with increasingly heavier set of weights.

Cricketing success did, as was hoped, follow. Shildon BR Cricket Club went on to win the Durham County League Cup, not just in 1955 but successfully defended the prize the following year. They had success too in the League Championship in 1962, 1966 and 1971 as well as carrying off the Horner Cup in 1964.

Aside from raising the prospects of the cricket team through the introduction of these splendid new sporting facilities, being part of the new national British Rail Staff Association brought new opportunities to compete on a regional and national basis. For example, the winter competitions that took place annually and encompassed competitive indoor games such as cribbage, individually and in pairs, darts for individual and teams, dominoes, whist, billiards and snooker. The players that were successful at branch and area finals were able to go on to compete at regional level, after which they were combined together in a team to represent their region in national finals.

Players representing Shildon Institute sometimes made the regional team such as on Saturday 19 April 1958 when Shildon branch players were part of a team at the North-East Region Winter Competitions Semi Finals and Finals at York.

Another regional contest, this time held in the summer and most likely as part of wider seasonal games, was the British Railways tug-of-war contest. A report in the Gateshead Post tells of a regional final held on Saturday 16 June 1956 where a team from Gateshead beat a much fancied Shildon team who had been the anticipated favourites on account of having been the much heavier team.

Springing a Leek

In 1954 a new Leek and Horticultural Society was formed in association with both the Institute and the BRSA, with an annual competitive show taking place in the Institute's Main Hall. Here prizes were awarded for those leeks, flowers and vegetables that were deemed by judges to be the most exceptional.

It's somewhat unsurprising that a passion for horticulture had thrived across Shildon. It was one of the most poplar cultural recreations right across industrial towns and villages of the region. But it is particularly heartening here given the fact that those early members of the Institute, of whom we have said much earlier in the book, had campaigned so arduously for allotment land for the railwaymen to tend.

By the 1950s there was no sign of that enthusiasm waning. Allotments were, by then, widely available right across the town. Many were on land rented out by the local authority, or else by the estate of Lord Eldon. However, the Institute and its members, through the prior generosity of the North Eastern Railway Company, had a portion of allotment land of their own to allocate. This was a parcel of land, shown on the original Institute deeds, to the rear of the Institute building on Redworth Road. It was bordered by Adamson Street to the east, Beresford Street to the west and the Urban District Boundary to the south. Beyond that were more allotments on Lord Eldon's land just west of All Saints Church.

Occasionally a special guest would be invited to present prizes. For example at the Institute's annual Flower and Vegetable Show on Saturday 28 September 1957, it was the serving Railway Queen, Teressa Boyden, from Peterborough, who opened the event and later awarded the Regional Cup for vegetables to Mr A Hopps and the cup for flowers to Mr A Parnaby.

Above: The gardeners vegetable exhibits are set out in the Institute hall, displayed in their respective sections in anticipation of judging.

Long standing Institute member Roz Langley, still a regular visitor today, remembers the Horticultural Shows at the Institute well from her childhood. She attended her first in around 1959 when she was just five years old. They were held annually in September, when the leeks would have been at their best. They were a tremendous spectacle and a truly sensory experience. The savoury scent of the leeks, onions and vegetables would hang in the air and there would be a display of vibrant colour from the chrysanthemums and buttonhole flowers.

A major motivation for participation in the various classes in these horticultural contests was the array of spectacular prizes on offer. Throughout the year the members of the society would contribute through regular subscriptions towards a prize fund. The Institute still possesses a small wooden box, labelled BRSA Leek Club, used to collect the contributions from the club members. This pot of prize money would then be invested in prizes, which Roz remembers as having been purchased, for some years at least, from Doggarts department store in nearby Bishop Auckland. The prizes themselves would be arranged on display at one end of the Institute's spacious main hall. Some of them would be large items of furniture, for example a wardrobe or an Ottoman chest.

The Leek and Horticultural Shows continued for several decades, and in later years were held on the Institute's first floor rather than the main hall. The Institute still retains a number of the trophies issued to the winners of the various classes in the horticultural competitions. They are each adorned with the names of each year's victorious gardener. They include a silver bowl awarded to the grower of the best collection of four dahlias, and shields for the winners of the most points in the flower and vegetable sections. By the beginning of the twenty-first century, enthusiasm for growing perfect outsized vegetables and magnificent flowers had waned, and several of the leading organisers retired or passed away. Consequently there were fewer competitive growers taking part and smaller prizes. Eventually participation fizzled out, not just at the Institute, but across the town and the region in general. Many leek clubs and shows in the area ultimately stopped being held as a consequence of the Covid pandemic of 2020 during which clubs were not permitted to meet. This resulted in prize funds not being built up so consequently there was no incentive to compete. Somehow many organisers, upon which these clubs depended, lost the will to get the competitions going again.

Alterations and Extension

Throughout the lifetime of the Institute's current building on Redworth Road a few physical changes have occurred, but not many. A keen observer might notice, after looking at the oldest photographs of the exterior, that the chimney pots which originally crowned the chimney stacks on the main roof have been removed and those chimneys themselves considerably shortened. When the Institute building was designed and built, coal was the staple fuel used across both urban and rural communities in the region. Having been mined in the area, it was readily available and in plentiful supply.

Other photographs, taken of the Institute building within a few days of it opening, show that rooms within had open fireplaces with mantelpieces. If you look around the building today you can see that almost every room still shows evidence of a chimney breast. Those photographs reveal that there was clearly also a network of pipes connecting iron radiators around the building. Beneath the Institute there is a cellar with a flue leading right up through the building to the roof and plenty of evidence to suggest that water for bathing, cleaning and the heating system was originally heated by a boiler here with heat produced by burning solid fuel. What happened to change that?

If you look across the rooftops of Shildon today you will notice that most of the buildings on the older streets also have chimney stacks, where many of the newer ones do not. You'll notice the general absence of plumes of chimney smoke across the town.

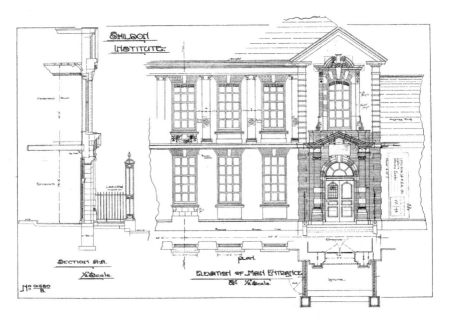

Above: One of the architect's original 1911 drawings of the Institute building design showing some detail of the original railings (left) as well as the decorative stonework.

A societal trend away from burning coal, coke and wood in towns commenced after the 1956 Clean Air Act, which was followed by a second Act in 1968. In reaction to by poor levels of public health in built-up areas, which was understood to have been a consequence of fire smoke, soot and smog, these Acts of Parliament gave local authorities in urban areas the power to prohibit householders and business owners from emitting smoke from chimneys. This shift in law and regulation nationally was probably a significant contributing factor in the boarding up of open fireplaces and removal of mantlepieces throughout the Institute building.

We know from later annual statements of accounts that the Institute's central heating system was also eventually converted from burning solid fuel to burning oil. This was in turn replaced by a gas boiler. The only remaining open fireplace in the building is in the former caretaker's accommodation on the second floor.

Another noticeable change over the decades concerns the courtyard and wall around the front and side of the building. The earliest photographs of the building, taken just as construction was concluding show considerably different perimeter railings to the ones you will see today. Mounted atop the wall, the original railings had supports that extended into the courtyard itself, a feature missing today. There were also ornate iron decorative arches, one placed before the main entrance, and a second similar gated one at the west end of the courtyard near the end of the main hall. These are also detailed on the architects original drawings.

It is thought, though not proven, that these original railings and decorative arches were a short-lived feature, and were removed during the years of the First World War as a contribution to metal collections to aid the war effort. Though this practice was more commonly done during the Second World War, we have photographic evidence that they had been removed before the Centenary Book was published 1933. By then poplar trees, and what seems to be a hedge, had been planted around the courtyard perimeter and look to have become well established. It is said locally that these trees were planted in remembrance of soldiers and sailors that gave their lives in the 1914-18 war. A later photograph, that we think to have been taken between the wars, shows the poplars standing taller than the Institute building itself and it's likely that they were felled not too long afterward, probably over concerns that their roots may otherwise have begun to affect stability of the perimeter wall or the exterior of the Institute building.

If, when visiting the Institute today, you take a close look at the capstones along the top of the wall, and especially the larger square ones where the wall ends near the main entrance, you can see where the original railings had been cut off. The square capstones have four stubs of metal each showing where the base of the decorative iron arches were set into the stonework. You'll also notice that the railings atop the walls have now been replaced to secure the perimeter. These were added to in more recent years when some well engineered gates were created and installed by Selwyn Jenkin, a member and Committee member with considerable practical engineering expertise.

Above: The Institute building on Redworth Road between the wars, showing the poplar trees planted in honour of the fallen. Note also the original chimney stacks and pots.

Alterations being carried out by members in this way was probably quite normal, given what the majority of the members did day to day in their jobs at the railway works. Not all, however, have been quite so elegant as the gates. Another noticeable post-war alteration is the somewhat crudely built fire escape mechanism on the Adamson Street end of the building that allows evacuation from the first floor. This functional, if unattractive, modification required conversion of one of the window apertures to serve as a fire exit doorway. It has been said that it was constructed by engineers from the railway works, probably in response to tightening fire regulations.

As well as making exterior alterations, the organisation also occasionally felt it necessary to reconfigure the interior. This usually happened as the members' needs and consequent usage of the building changed with the passage of time. The Redworth Road building, large as it was, offered plenty of scope for rearrangement, and though it may have been ideal by design when it opened in 1913, there were strong views later, among the members and committee, that some rearrangements had become necessary.

A committee meeting was held on 2 September 1957 to agree and itemise suggestions that should be pursued, and to discuss how any changes could be achieved financially.

Perhaps unsurprisingly, looking back to the past and knowing how the institute has evolved, the first of the minuted enhancements was that the cellar beneath the Institute should be altered to enable the storage and sale of draught beer. This would necessitate the erection of a new partition wall within the cellar, the creation of a new entrance via the stockroom along with creation of a chute down to the cellar from outside to enable delivery of coke directly to the boiler room.

The next two suggestions minuted were that the Billiard Room on the lower floor, originally the Reading Room but which we now know as the Members Bar, should become a lounge for members. This would be given a new external entrance opening onto Adamson Street, which has since become a ground floor fire escape. The new lounge would require a bar counter to be built to enable drinks to be served. A new opening was to be added between this new lounge and the room adjacent to enable staff to attend to both rooms, and new beer pumps were to be acquired. Furthermore, new bar furnishings would be ordered, including new plywood flooring, linoleum, pelmets, curtains and nineteen black legged tables with yellow formica tops. Some of those tables are still in use today at the Institute. An additional enhancement was the creation of one hundred feet of wall seating.

At the same time, the room that had, up to that point, been serving as a Library and Games Room would be repurposed as the new Billiard Room, with the large billiard tables being moved back upstairs to where they had originally been when the building originally opened. The Reading Room would become the Library where the Institute's collection of books would be re-housed. And part of the new Billiard Room would be re-designated as being for use as a Reading Room. This was a significant re-arrangement of the building.

By the time of a special meeting on 11 March 1958, estimated costs had been acquired for all of the anticipated work. The alterations would also involve a considerable amount of redecoration and costs were also provided for further changes to improve lighting. The Secretary reported that the costs of the alterations had been estimated to amount to just short of £1,800. This was a considerably significant sum of money in those days.

A few amendments to the original intentions were also communicated at the special meeting. It was suggested that the present door to the stockroom should be sealed up, with a new entrance being added instead from the central passage running through the ground floor of the building. The new chute for coke delivery would also be used for removal of the spent ashes from heating the boiler, so that they did not need to be carried up the cellar steps and out through the first floor of the building. A new partition was also to be placed at the top of the cellar steps to enable empty barrels and crates to be stored and reduce transmission of dust from the cellar to public areas of the building.

It was also suggested at that same meeting that the coke fired boiler for heating should be replaced by an oil fired boiler. The suggestion was deemed a step too far on this occasion and set aside as a future aspiration, which we understand to have come to fruition some years later.

With regard to paying for the alterations, the Secretary reported to his committee colleagues that he had spoken to a Mr Barrett at the York offices, and that he understood from the ensuing conversation that the Shildon Institute was to receive a return of around £995 from British Rail, and would be eligible to apply for a loan from the British Rail Staff Association for the remainder.

At a subsequent meeting on 27 March, committee members learned that the amount they would receive from British Rail at York was to be far less than they had anticipated, being only £483. They passed a motion that the best approach would be to apply to the British Rail Staff Association for a loan of the full sum of £1,800. At the same meeting it was noted that at a proposal from Mr M Stanthorpe of the committee, requesting serious consideration of the provision of ladies toilets at the Institute, had been omitted from the minutes, and it was agreed that this should be kept in hand and carried out.

The most significant external alteration to the building throughout its history, came in 1966. Up until that year, the caretaker or steward of the Institute and his family had occupied the purpose built accommodation which occupied the space beneath the roof; effectively a second floor of the building. Roz Langley remembers visiting her childhood friend Val Storey (now Bunting) there in the early sixties. Val's parents were Steward and Stewardess at the time. Roz recalls that the flat seemed quite small and very dark inside, though it had windows to the front and rear. Val herself remembers having to climb lots of stairs to get to the flat, and that her father struggled with the stairs in later years.

Around the mid-nineteen-sixties the Institute Committee had decided to make practical structural changes to resolve a handful of perceived issues. The building's use had shifted further away form its original purpose as a library and reading room. Newspapers were being delivered daily to most homes and books were more accessible through the introduction of public libraries across the nation. Low cost books were freely available. During the British Rail Staff Association era, more emphasis became placed on social activity, and an increased capability and capacity to stock and sell drinks. This latest reconfiguration of the building saw the introduction of a dedicated bar serving area as a building extension on the rear exterior of the main hall, along with an additional brick built extension to the rear of the building to accommodate improved internal toilet facilities and a new ground floor beer cellar. There was good news for the Storey family too, as a new, more modern, flat roofed stewards apartment with more windows was built directly on top of the new beer cellar.

Annual statements of account and balance sheets show that though the Institute was on a relatively sound financial footing in those days, with a healthy reserve balance, these significant building alterations were also paid for by entering into a loan agreement with British Rail Engineering Limited.

Last of the Railway Queens

On 22 November 1974 the Institute at Shildon had been prepared to receive a special visit by the Railway Queen for 1974/75. We explained earlier that, as part of the celebrations of the Railway Centenary in 1925, an annual contest had commenced to elect a national Railway Queen from hopeful candidates representing railway towns across the operating regions. By 1974 decisions had been made that the Railway Queen for 1975 would be the last, bringing this fifty year old tradition to a close. The finals of the contest that year took place, in time honoured manner, during September at Belle Vue, Manchester. At around the same time the eyes of rail enthusiasts were already looking toward to north-east, and to Shildon, in anticipation of the upcoming steam passenger railway 150 year anniversary the following year. There was an appetite to do something to acknowledge Shildon's place in that event. The Committee of Shildon Railway Institute recognised that their hall was, of course, too small to host the finals of the Railway Queen competition. It was still possible, however, for the queen to pay a visit for a special 'crowning' ceremony.

The Committee had once again prepared and planned meticulously for the event, preparing a programme featuring advertisements from supporting businesses in the locality, photographs taken by the Institute's Photographic Society, and the programme of entertainment for the evening. This put on sale to members and visitors for five pence.

Other special guests had been invited to be present. These included the former 1970-71 Railway Queen Lynette Skilbeck, née

Storr, from York and Shildon's own candidate for the 1974 Railway Queen contest, Janice Wharton, who worked as a clerk in the Computer Bureau at the BR offices at Stooperdale in Darlington.

Above: Brenda Tomlinson, the 1975, and last, British Railway Queen in the Hackworth Lounge on her visit to the Institute at Shildon.

Celebrations commenced at seven o'clock, with members and guests being treated to 'taped music' before dancing commenced at eight o'clock, followed by a chance to watch footage of the competition finalists. A brief twenty-minute break for bingo was followed by more dancing until ten-thirty, whereupon there was an opportunity to watch part of the ceremony involving presentation of a past railway queen. At quarter to ten the assemblage settled down to watch the winner, Miss Brenda Tomlinson from Manchester, being crowned. After this, there was more dancing followed by a final brief interval in which the new

new Railway Queen formally opened the recently redecorated concert hall.

Above: The plaque unveiled by Brenda Tomlinson to mark the beginning of the S&DR 150th anniversary celebrations.

A further additional duty undertaken by the Railway Queen that evening involved unveiling a small plaque at the Institute to mark the start of celebrations of the 150th Anniversary of the opening of the Stockton & Darlington Railway, heralding the exciting festivities in the year ahead. This plaque is still in its place at the Institute, affixed above the members' bar. The year ahead would surely prove a very exciting one for Shildon and its people.

150th S&DR Anniversary Celebrations

The year 1975 was one that would live long in the memory of Shildon folk. At the end of August a grand ten-day exhibition of historic locomotives and rolling stock was going to be hosted at the Shildon Works site, which many forget was the birthplace of many historic early locomotives long before it became more famous for its wagons. This upcoming unique railway spectacular would surpass the scale and grandeur of one held by the LNER for the Institute's centenary in 1933. It would culminate in a Grand Steam

Cavalcade on 31 August wherein all of the locomotives would be paraded along the route of the Stockton & Darlington Railway line towards Darlington.

Much has been written in other books about this celebration, so we shall not say too much about the cavalcade or its impact on Shildon that year, though we shall return to it. It was however unusual for Shildon to be in the spotlight at a major Stockton and Darlington Railway anniversary celebration.

When the first of these major celebrations occurred, in 1875, to celebrate fifty years, organisers almost bypassed Shildon altogether. In Darlington, the council invested an equivalent of what would be £80,000 today on decorations, illuminations and triumphal arches, with the North Eastern Railway contributing five times that amount. The statue of Joseph Pease, the Institute's first patron, was unveiled in Darlington's Market Place. Speeches were held and bands played. An exhibition of locomotives was staged at the Darlington engine sheds, and the Lord Mayor of London made a visit to tour the exhibits before attending a banquet of the finest French cuisine for 900 dignitaries. The culmination of festivities was a firework display by experts from the Crystal Palace at London.

Shildon waited patiently until 9 November that year when a tea was held at the old Institute on Station Street. The wealthy Darlington investors, the Peases, attended, as did John Wesley Hackworth presided over by the Institute's John Glass. The latter spoke in defence of Shildon which had been much maligned in an article in the Northern Echo. Daniel Adamson, unable to attend in person, had sent a letter, which was read out. A modest display of fireworks closed the evening.

The next major milestone occurred in 1925, that being of course, the centenary of the Stockton and Darlington Railway. This the first in which a steam cavalcade was arranged, which was staged in the presence of the Duke and Duchess of York, not in Shildon, but on track east of Darlington between Urlay Nook and Oak Tree.

Again everything centred on Darlington, which was swathed in pennants, streamers and bunting suspended by crimson and gold pylons all the way from Bank Top Station to Faverdale. A great exhibition was again staged at the company headquarters in Stooperdale. In Stockton, also somewhat neglected that year, a commemorative plaque was unveiled.

Shildon's planning for the Centenary, started at the end of 1923, and intended to work towards unveiling of a statue of Timothy Hackworth on the Recreation Ground. This the local centenary committee hoped to unveil on 26 September, the day before the anniversary date on which everyone would have gone to

Darlington to experience the wonders there. The Hackworth statue was created by Messrs Fattorini of Leeds, with much of the financial contribution toward the cost being made by the railway company, some money added by Mr Ferens of Hull, and the rest having been raised directly by Shildon people.

By October, over a month after the Shildon celebration had been hoped to take place, the fund was still sixty pounds short, which was not an insignificant amount in 1925. It wasn't until 5 December that a parade of children was able to be marched from Shildon's Market Place to the recreation ground for the grand unveiling. Three-thousand-five-hundred lucky children in the town received a special commemorative mug, and the school, situated on Byerley Road, was renamed in honour of Timothy Hackworth.

Earlier that year, on 4 July, in a separate moment of centenary jubilation, eight railwaymen from the LNER rang out all five-thousand-one-hundred-and-twenty changes of the "Kent Treble in Bb Major" on the church bells of St John's – which lasted three hours and twenty minutes. Almost enough bell ringing to possibly cause even Hackworth himself to stir.

The "jewel in the crown" of the 1925 celebration had been the cavalcade of locomotives and rolling stock, billed at the time as "six miles of interest, a spectacle which cannot recur". Of course, as we now know, it did recur, and that happened in 1975.

This time, for once, the world's attention was focused on Shildon. For this new cavalcade, a special working replica of Stephenson's No. 1 Engine, better known today as "Locomotion No. 1", had been built at a cost of £40,000. The construction project was overseen by the aptly named Locomotion Trust, and the construction was mostly undertaken by a group of organisations from around the North East that specialised in training engineering skills. To see this new replica lead the grand parade would be far more moving than witnessing the poor aged veteran original being pushed along the line with its once proud head of steam being simulated by the smoke from the burning of an oily rag.

That 1975 cavalcade at Shildon, honouring the 150th anniversary of the opening of the Stockton & Darlington Railway, was only possible because of the available capacity to host and exhibit the locomotives at the Shildon Works site. There was a great deal of excitement and anticipation as the locomotives set out in chronological order from oldest to newest, passing the historic Masons Arms and proceeding east toward Heighington. From there some locomotives returned to Shildon on the down line, while others continued onward to Darlington from where they could return to their respective home depots by road or rail.

Stands had been erected along the cavalcade route to accommodate spectators, and it seemed that every possible vantage point along the route was taken by an eager crowd keen to see this once in a lifetime spectacle.

The leading exhibit in this grand parade had to be, of course, the replica Locomotion engine towing a chaldron wagon and forcett coach. Other engines followed at two minute intervals, by over thirty historic locomotives in all, most from the steam era and representing most of the major rail companies operating around the regions of the country through the railway age. Each locomotive steadily crawled along the line at no more than five miles per hour, while the crowds along the route took photographs, watched and waved. Some even captured the moment on eight millimetre cine film. The nostalgic ramble through progress in locomotive design continued right through to the latest advance in rail passenger travel, a British Railways High Speed Train bringing up the rear of the procession.

Though the grand exhibition and procession was the principal formally organised, and rather expensive, centrepiece of the 1975 Shildon celebrations, there were many other aspects of that year's celebrations that had been organised by different sections of the community. The Railway Institute's programme of events to mark the moment included an exhibition of railway art that had been painted by the noted artist John Wigston.

John Edwin Wigston was born in Redhill, in Surrey in 1939. He trained in horticulture and served in the RAF before a career that had brought him north to a job at the ICI chemical works on Teesside. John had a fascination with railways and transport, and had begun channelling this through his passion for painting. He had studied art at evening classes in Hartlepool, and by 1970 had sufficient a portfolio of work as to be the subject of an exhibition at Hartlepool's Gray Gallery. This was the first of many showings of his work, which attracted attention around the region, and led to his being engaged for the 1975 exhibition at the Railway Institute.

His paintings of the pioneering era of steam railways are vivid and atmospheric and conjure up a real sense of wonder at what would, in their day, have been engineering marvels. One painting from 1975 depicts Hackworth's "Royal George" locomotive, the engine that finally proved the viability of steam power over horse power, standing outside the engineer's own house. Another painted in 1974 for the 150th Anniversary, entitled "The Stockton and Darlington Railway" is a stunning montage composition featuring Hackworth, and both George and Robert Stephenson, as well as "Locomotion No. 1", a model of Hackworth's "Royal George" and a horse leading four chaldron wagons over the Gaunless Bridge. It was also one of Wigston's paintings of Locomotion No. 1 that adorned the front cover of the official Souvenir Guide Book published by the Joint Committee for Stockton & Darlington Railway 150 Celebrations.

Anther celebratory feature of the anniversary year was a grand carnival and fancy dress parade through the town, held on the August Bank Holiday, which was Monday 25 August. The parade formed up on Middleton Road at 2pm and wound its way around the principal roads through the town.

Shops and businesses around Shildon received a huge, though brief, boost in trade from the 1975 celebrations. Opportunities to 'cash-in' on the sudden interest presented themselves   in many forms. Some folk with land were able to charge inbound visitors for car parking. Others stocked up on souvenirs to sell. Among those items created in tribute and made available to purchase were, almost unbelievably, celebratory cans of locomotive steam. It was made clear on the product's packaging that the cans were, of course, empty and that they were something of a 'tongue in cheek' souvenir.

From the end of August right through to Saturday 27 September, a significant programme of minor sideshow events and activities took place, organised by the town's various societies and churches. These were itemised in advance in a special event programme distributed to the public. Many were hosted by the Institute, either at its building on Redworth Road or at its sister site, the BRSA Sports Field.

The Institute events advertised in the community programme were as follows:

Sun 24 Aug 1975 - a Five-a-side Cricket Knockout
competition for railway town teams - at the sports field.

Mon 25 Aug 1975 - Northumberland & Durham Foreign
Bird Society Invitation Show - at the Institute building.

Tue 26 Aug 1975 - Old Tyme Dance - with dancers in
period costume - at the Institute building.

Thu 28 Aug 1975 - BREL Foremen's Association Dance
- at the Institute building.

Fri 29 Aug 1975 - Farewell Celebrity Show - at the
Institute building.

Sat 30 Aug 1975 - Grand Open Show and Sports with home produce, flowers, photography, arts & crafts, tug of war, five-a-side - at the sports field.

Sat 30 Aug 1975 - BRSA Leek & Horticultural Show Day 1 - at the Institute building.

Sat 30 Aug 1975 - Jubilee Dance - at the Institute building.

Sun 31 Aug 1975 - BRSA Leek & Horticultural Show Day 2 - at the Institute building.

Sat 30 Aug 1975 - Grand Cavalcade Dance - at the Institute building.

Sat 27 Sep 1975 - Grand Fireworks Display and Bonfire supplied by Brock's Fireworks Limited of London who provided the firework display for the first Railway Jubilee in 1875 - at the sports field.

Looking closer at the last of these events, I found it quite remarkable that Brock's Fireworks of London were still trading one hundred years after the first jubilee fireworks organised by the Institute in 1875, and even more so to learn that at the time of my writing this, a further forty-eight years on, it is a brand that it still in business. Perhaps we might look forward to seeing more of Brock's fireworks organised by the Institute to mark the upcoming railway bicentenary in 2025.

Institute member Roz Langley recalls something further about the time of the railway celebrations which is that for a few days the Institute opened up a rarely used kitchen to offer simple meals at the Institute. The dish on offer was something of a culinary staple around pubs and clubs at that time. A 'basket meal' of chicken served on a bed of chips in a paper lined basket container. It was a popular inexpensive dining out option during the late 1960s and right throughout the 1970s.

To remember the year's festivities, the Institute also acquired specially produced trays and pens commemorating Shildon and the Stockton & Darlington Railway.

As for John Wigston, he went on to become an artist in residence to the National Railway Museum, based in York, and selected works from his lifetime of painting have been the subject of further exhibitions at Shildon's Locomotion museum, with the first such having run from July to September 2013.

A Town Under Siege

The mid-1980s proved a pivotal point in the story not only of the Institute, but also Shildon itself. Prior to this decade the British Rail Engineering Limited (BREL) Works at Shildon had been thriving. While a town's industry thrives, its local economy thrives. But what might happen when if doesn't?

Rather like Shildon's pioneering railway engineering history, the story of the events and decision imposed upon the staff at Shildon Works throughout the nineteen-eighties is better documented in detail in other books, or resources available online, than I shall offer you here, but I do feel it necessary to write a little about what was happening during that period, purely as context for what happened next to the Institute and its members.

We begin in 1962 with a wave of changes that would affect Shildon Works. This was the year that British Rail created British Rail Workshops Limited as a division. This incorporated all of its works locations. The new division was headquartered in Derby, but included works at Ashford, Crewe, Derby, Doncaster, Eastleigh, Horwich, Temple Mills, Swindon, Wolverton and York as well as Shildon. As part of an associated modernisation drive, the Shildon works received new equipment to enable it to focus particularly on repair of British Rail built wagons. This capability was expanded in 1970 to enable repair of other types of wagons from abroad.

As well as its wagon building operation, which produced among other types the Presflo cement wagons, Freightliners and merry-go-round coal hoppers, the works now had capacity to repair eight-hundred wagons per week. The reorganised workshops division became British Rail Engineering Limited on 1 January 1970 as a consequence of the 1968 Transport Act.

On 4 May 1979 a Conservative Government came into power at Westminster, under the leadership of Margaret Thatcher. Thatcher's personal political philosophy and economic policy was built, in significant part, upon a belief that nationalised industries should be privatised, and that the power and influence of trade unions should be greatly reduced. It would be a mistake to believe that it was only Thatcher holding this belief. Throughout the nationalised rail era several key industrialists had written of that perceived need to re-privatise Britain's railways, claiming that nationalisation starved the country, and of course themselves, of opportunities. Even today, Conservatives and their wealthy backers, many of whom profit from privatisation, continue to oppose state owned industries and operations.

Above: Photograph taken at the Institute, thought to have been of a meeting as part of the campaign to save Shildon Works during the 1980s.

Thatcher's election victory placed her in a position where she at last had significant power to progress a programme of privatisation. Those that had funded her election campaign, along with more than thirteen and a half million people that had voted for her party of MPs, were now cheering her on from the sidelines. What ensued was biggest programme of national de-industrialisation in British history, and a large scale cut-price sell-off of nationalised industries to private investors. Britons were told repeatedly that governments were not able to run business as effectively as the private sector; a statement which now resonates with some irony given how decades later so much of our own national transport infrastructure is run by subsidiaries of the state owned transport bodies of other countries. At the time of writing this book, Germany's state-owned Deutsche Bahn, Italy's state-owned Trenitalia, France's state-owned SNCF, Holland's state-owned Abellio and Chinese Hong Kong's state-owned MTR all now run, and draw profit from, parts of Britain's rail services.

Back in the eighties, the Government's many privatisation objectives included a desire to slim down the nation's rail engineering operation to a point where what was left would be ripe for selling off to a private investment company or business. This, of course, included British Rail Engineering Limited. The executives of BREL, as employees of the state, were given their directive accordingly.

For Shildon, the first announcement of an intention to close the Shildon Works came on 23 April 1982, a time when around two-thousand-six-hundred people were employed at the Shildon Works. Rumours of the announcement had been circulating for around eight days beforehand, and a small pre-emptive demonstration had taken place outside the British Rail headquarters in London.

The National Union of Railwaymen (NUR), under General Secretary Sid Weighell, mobilised to campaign against the closure, and on 29 April a mile long march, comprising of about five-thousand people, headed by MP Derek Foster and MEP Roland Boyes, snaked through the town to a rally at the football ground on Dean Street. This was followed on 25 May by a demonstration wherein six-hundred people travelled by train to London to deliver six-hundred-and-thirty letters to British Rail's chairman, Sir Peter Parker, before lobbying influential Members of Parliament. Another large rally back in Shildon took place on 29 May, at which several prominent politicians of the day tried to offer rousing speeches.

The working men of Shildon, however, sensed that despite the bravado of their representatives and politicians, the writing was on the wall for Shildon Works. There were reports of some men drifting away from the rally as the speeches progressed. Sid Weighell claimed later in 1990 that he sensed the Shildon union men, compared to NUR members overall, were a "bit subdued," and "maybe a bit too accommodating". In hindsight it could be argued that they were right to feel sceptical. A hard-nosed Tory Prime Minister on a mission to prove that the influence of the trade union movement could be broken, was never going to listen to their voices, or to relent in the slightest.

There was, however, a temporary reprieve when, on 4 June, British Rail announced a postponement in the decision to close the works. This intermission was believed to be, in part, due to a need to produce wagons for the recently announced Channel Tunnel, another of Margaret Thatcher's flagship projects. Significant redundancies were still communicated to the workforce as being necessary. Consequently, no new apprentices were taken on, but the works remained open for a while at least.

The final intention to close the works in 1984 was formally communicated on 18 February 1983. As that year progressed, Shildon workers were offered an enhanced redundancy package, softening the resistance of many.

On Saturday 28 April 1984, as part of a wider visit to the region, particularly to attend a May Day Rally at Stockton, the then leader of the Labour Party, the official Parliamentary Opposition, Neil Kinnock paid a visit to the Institute. By this time a reported seventeen-hundred workers had already been laid off from Shildon Works, and a further thousand redundancies were expected. Kinnock addressed a group of workers inside the Institute, and congratulated them for putting up a magnificent fight to save their livelihoods. He claimed to be "sorry from the bottom of his being" that he was unable to bring them good news. He expressed that their "unique level of skill and commitment had been rewarded by the closing of the gates," and that the "Government considers that whole areas of the country can just be discarded, and can't distinguish between slimming and starvation."

Shildon's works formally closed once and for all on 30 June 1984. The tracks that had passed through since its founding as the world's very first rail industry centre began to be lifted and removed even before the closure date. The Northern Echo of 25 June 1984 perfectly summed up the moment in this one grave paragraph:

> The last rites have started as Shildon Wagon Works' proud 150-year history grinds slowly to a halt. The doomed works are now echoing to the sound of the mechanical digger as the old tracks (connecting the works to the lines at Shildon station) are ripped from the ground. The remnants of a once mighty workforce looked solemnly on and knew there was no going back.

Throughout this period there was a gradual partial exodus of men and families away from Shildon. Pending orders were redistributed from Shildon away to Doncaster primarily, and other remaining BREL locations around the country. Sensing the industrial vacuum that was being created in the North-East of England, where other industrial centres, including nearby Consett's once famous steel works, were being dismantled, many Shildon men who had known no other occupation followed the work to those other places. Some would return, while others would not. The resulting economic decline created a shockwave that is still being felt by the community almost forty years later.

But what relevance was this to Shildon's unique and historic Railway Institute, and the BRSA Sports Ground that had become its sister site in 1955?

Fragmentation

The impact was not immediate, but it was clear that, as with the works site, British Rail Engineering Limited wanted to dispose of social facilities it held as assets. There were numerous options available as to how this might be done, and for those assets in Shildon it would be down to the membership of the Shildon Branch of the British Rail Staff Association to decide which direction they wanted to pursue. Options were explored at a meeting between senior committee members and representatives of the British Rail Eastern Region, BREL and the British Rail Property Board at the Moat Hotel, in York, and were later presented to Institute members at a special subject meeting on Tuesday June 12 1984.

The following four options were presented to members:

Option 1 - That the premises and property (i.e. the Institute building and the sports ground) be transferred from the ownership of BREL to become the property of the British Rail Board Eastern Region - and for the branch to carry on as a properly constituted branch of the BRSA within the Eastern Region.

Option 2 - That a new private organisation would be created, and ownership of both the Institute building and the sports ground would be transferred from BREL to that new organisation.

Option 3 - That the sports ground continue under the BRSA under the ownership of the British Rail Broad Eastern Region, but a new private organisation would be created to take ownership and control of the Institute building.

Option 4 - That the Institute building would continue under the BRSA under the ownership of the British Rail Broad Eastern Region, but a new private organisation would be created to take ownership and control of the sports ground.

We can be thankful at least that none of the options considered included outright closure, demolition and sale of the land and buildings for profit. Members were provided with the advantages and disadvantages of each approach to consider. For the sports ground, a key consideration was whether the facility could continue without the financial sports ground assistance that the British Rail Staff Association provided annually, which was at that time over five and a half thousand pounds. It was also uncertain whether anyone would be willing to become involved in running a private organisation to take care of the sports ground. An additional consideration was that, through the BRSA, the facilities at branches benefited from a significant nationwide discount on the purchase of beer to sell to members. This would be forfeited if the Institute, or the sports ground, or both, chose to go their own way. If the branch left the BRSA it would also no longer be eligible to compete in British Rail sporting contests.

Another consideration in the report presented to members was that other social organisations and facilities in the town had already started to struggle to survive as a result of both the economic dip and the exodus of families to other towns. There was also a concern regarding the Institute and sports ground losing their British Rail identity.

A perceived opportunity on the part of the Institute though, was that for the first time in its history the members might be able to take full ownership of the premises. This was a luxury that had not been possible throughout the preceding one hundred and fifty-one years. If this were to happen, it would bring the power of self determination over property, but also the daunting full responsibility for its maintenance.

The committee of the BRSA Shildon Branch presented members with a recommendation to pursue option 1 and to remain part of British Rail Staff Association under the BR Eastern Region. Not everyone agreed, and when the decision was made by a ballot of members on 20 June 1984 the outcome was that the preferred option was Option 3, that the Institute would strike out on its own. Under this option the Institute building and land would be transferred to the membership of the Institute for a minimal fee.

Had the Institute members chosen to remain with the Eastern Region of the British Railways Staff Association the situation would soon have changed anyway, for only six years later, in 1990, that organisation separated to become the fully autonomous National Association of Railway Clubs. There was no place in the British Rail structure for a society, focused on social benefits while the Government were sectorising British Rail and preparing its divisions to be sold to private investors.

With the Institute now committed to becoming fully independent of any railway company for the first time in its already long life, the committee of the new body met for the first time on 24 July 1984 to reconsider reconstitution.

Throughout its history the Institute had always had a senior and respected local railway figure acting as its President. This tradition began at the very outset in 1833 with the instatement of

Timothy Hackworth. At that July meeting, the committee decided to approach Alan Dunkley of Derby, then the Personnel Director of British Rail Engineering Limited, with a request that he accept the honorary position of President. They wrote to him on 30 July 1984 and he wrote back to confirm that he would be pleased to accept the responsibility. There was no specific description communicated of what was expected of Dunkley in that role.

With the Institute having been an integral part of the British Rail Staff Association, and frequented mainly by BREL employees, Dunkley, a senior figure in the industry, would have been many members' ideal choice for President for the newly independent Institute. He was well known by rail engineering workers nationally, although throughout the nineteen-eighties his name was more often seen in association with bad-news stories in the national and rail industry press; such as announcements of scaled back operations and redundancies at Ashford, Horwich, Shildon, Derby, Swindon, Wolverhampton, Doncaster and York. Nonetheless, he must have created sufficiently good impression in Shildon to have been afforded the honour of being offered presidency.

By the beginning of 1987, Dunkley moved to a new post within British Rail as Project Director for the network of British Rail Maintenance Limited (BRML) workshops. BREL lasted only a few more years until 1992 when it was bought by the Swiss-Swedish ABB transport corporation. BRML was privatised not long afterwards, with the various operations being carved up and purchased by separate private concerns by 1995.

We don't know a great deal about Alan Dunkley's life after the final sell-off, such as when he finally retired from work. There is no remaining evidence of any ongoing communication between him and members of the Institute committee. We do, however, know that he lived in Etwall, Derbyshire with his wife Barbara, and that they had two sons, Ian and Neil. He passed away peacefully at home on 4 April 2006.

Despite this passing, Dunkley's name has curiously appeared as President on each Annual Statement presented to the members at the Annual General Meeting each year since, as though nobody knew he had died, or given thought to the matter. At the time of writing the Institute has neither President nor Vice-Presidents in position, though this may change in future.

It was at that same inaugural meeting of evolved Institute that the proposal was made to introduce the concept of qualified free 'life-membership' for any members who had paid for their membership for at least 20 consecutive years.

In preparation for one of the meetings relating to this breakaway from the British Rail Staff Association, Secretary Brian

Above: Alan Dunkley (left), Personnel Director of British Rail Engineering Limited, a Derby man who was appointed president of the Institute in 1984 and whose name has appeared as President on annual balance sheets to this day, despite his passing in 2006.

Bulleyment made handwritten notes for what he felt he needed to say. These offer some insight in to the reasons for deciding to make the break.

> "First let it be perfectly clear that the management board of the Institute did not desire to come out of BRSA, but we did feel very strongly that since considerable capital had been invested by members who frequent the Institute that if the title deeds were available they should be held in trust at the Railway Institute. This position BRSA cannot accept.
>
> At the Institute we feel it would be a disaster if we lost the marvellous facilities we currently enjoy so we must tonight make the correct choice. We accept the need and logic for the sports field staying within BRSA and all it offers but the Institute is quite

different and as it can be self-supporting it would appear that a golden opportunity to have the best of both worlds for our members."

He went on to say in conclusion:

"We sincerely hope that we can afford to keep our wonderful facilities, but we have to think ahead, and Option 3 gives us an asset that cannot be taken away, but may never again be offered."

Above: Alan Dunkley (front row, 4th from right) of BREL hands over the deeds to the Institute building and land to Brian Bulleyment and the committee as part of the transfer of ownership from British Rail.

The Institute appointed Hewitt Brown Humes and Hare, of Bishop Auckland, as its solicitors to handle the conveyancing of the building to the new organisation. The solicitors also drew the committee's attention to the Friendly Societies Act as a path forward for the new organisation format, after the Institute had rejected a suggestion of joining the Club and Institute Union (CIU).

A trust was formed comprising elected representatives of the committee - these were John Tweddle, John Lithgoe, Ken Brass, Barry Doughty, George Bellas and Bob Foster. Plans were made for British Rail Engineering Limited to hand over the title deeds to the Railway Institute building at a special celebratory event on the evening of 23 August 1985.

That event commenced at 6:45pm for pre-drinks, followed by a buffet dinner and dancing to the Clive Collins Band. The ceremonial handover of deeds took place at 9pm with a speech of thanks on behalf of the Institute. Further dancing followed.

The Boxing Club Move In

As we explained earlier, Shildon Amateur Boxing Club has had a presence in the town since its founding in 1903, and it lays claim to being the second oldest such club in the United Kingdom. In that time, as we mentioned earlier, it has also been nomadic, having had several bases of operation. Its goal has always been stated as encouraging and supporting youngsters, from age eight upwards, to reach their potential through the discipline and art of boxing, and it has been very successful at that, having produced over one-hundred national finalists.

The club originally trained its young boxers in what is known as Timothy Hackworth's Soho Engine Shed, but is more properly known as Kilburn's Warehouse. This arrangement continued right through until 1979 whereupon they left that premises under an impression that the then Sedgefield District Council, at that time the middle tier of local authority governing the area, were going to provide them with a dedicated training gym of their own. This expectation failed to materialise, leading to the club moving into the former Shildon Works canteen building which still stands near the Masons Arms today, and later, when the works closed, to an old maintenance department building.

From there, the club moved again, spending some time training away from the town, at Middlestone Moor, before making a return to Shildon to use the concert room at New Shildon Workingmen's Club. That arrangement ended when that club closed its doors for the final time before its demolition in 2002, whereupon the boxing club moved to Sunnydale School for a short period. The club then reached out to local councillors for assistance in finding a home, to no avail, and even contacted journalists at the Northern Echo to place a public appeal.

Their temporary accommodation problems continued until August 2004 when boxing club chairman Tom Taylor met with the Institute's Secretary, Brian Bulleyment, and others from the Institute Committee with a proposal.

The first floor of the Railway Institute building had fallen into disuse by the beginning of the twenty-first century, so was entirely vacant. Taking it over would require a little work, which men associated with the boxing club were prepared to carry out, but otherwise it would make an ideal home base for the venerable club.

Above: Aaron Huberry of Shildon Amateur Boxing Club, the club's 99th national champion, with coach John Heighington in the boxing gym in the Institute's first floor.

The Institute Committee met to discuss the proposal, and agreed that it would make sense for the two organisations to collaborate in this way. Bulleyment wrote to the secretary of the boxing club on 2 September 2004, outlining the basis of an agreement.

The Institute would lease the first floor of its building to the boxing club for a period of twenty-five years. The letter outlined the rates that would be due to the institute, which were quite charitable, and several conditions, which included that the Institute itself would also continue to operate from the same address. The boxing club would have exclusive use of the building's first floor.

The club moved in soon after, erecting boxing rings and installing training equipment. Though training at the Institute, competitive bouts hosted by the boxing club continued to be held at Shildon Civic Hall, it being of larger breadth than the Institute's main hall and deemed to be a more appropriate venue.

This partnership between the Institute and the boxing club endured for fifteen years, and we will return to it in an upcoming chapter.

100 Years on Redworth Road

The second decade of the twenty-first century brought two celebrations for the Institute. The first was a marking of the diamond jubilee of the Shildon Railway Institute Modern Sequence Dance Club.

This marvellous little society had been inaugurated in the hall at the Institute on 5 September 1951, at which time members could pay a single shilling to come along and dance to Tommy Smurthwaite and his band. Such dance clubs were once extremely popular in the region, but by 2013 the club at Shildon was one of very few still running. Its membership had diminished to around fifty dancers from a one-time peak of about one-hundred-and-thirty.

The dance club had already celebrated fifty years of existence back on 4 September 2001, with a special 'gold' themed evening; an event that had been attended and reported upon by Mike Amos of the Northern Echo. In the interview piece, members worried that 'old time dancing' was dwindling. They need not have worried, for ten years later the club was still going steadily.

The 60th anniversary celebration took place on Tuesday 13 September 2011, with a specially made cake, sporting a dancing couple as a centrepiece, and an added visual spectacle of a dancing display by the Dianne White Academy of Dance. A buffet had also been prepared for the dancers by kindly ladies from the Methodist Church. The anniversary party was widely reported in the local press, articles featuring a brief interview with the then secretary of the dancing club, Lillian Storey. A special group photograph, featuring all of the members present, captured the spirit of the moment.

We are proud and pleased to inform the reader at this point that the club continued to enjoy its seventieth anniversary in 2021 and was still active throughout the Institute's 190th year, bringing elegant grace to the dance floor in the hall every Tuesday night.

Above: Members of the Institute's Modern Sequence Dance Club celebrate their 60th anniversary in the main hall of the Institute during 2011.

The second of these celebrations related to the fact that, in February 2013, the Institute had been resident at its Redworth Road building for exactly 100 years. The staff and committee decided that a small celebration was in order, so Stewardess, Hazel Johnson, made arrangements to display a small exhibition of maps and photographs. To do this members were asked to contribute photographs from their own collections which were then enlarged by photocopier and mounted on the walls to be admired.

The collection depicted many aspects of the day to day business of the Institute including sports teams of years gone by, groups of committee men, members of the amateur boxing club, and a magnificent portrait of the Shildon LNER Works Silver Band from 1937, resplendent in their uniforms, depicted with their instruments and trophies upstairs in the Institute.

The photographs also included images of the building throughout the years, starting with one from a postcard of Hildyard Terrace before the Institute building had been constructed; leafy trees and a green occupying the space where the grand building now stands. Another showed the committee of 1913 arranged in three rows outside the Institute's main front entrance, also clearly showing the decorative ironwork of the original entrance arch under which members had to pass to enter the building. Another depicted the building toward the late 1940s, surrounded by the poplar trees that had been planted in remembrance of the members that fell in World War One. The most recent of the photographic portraits of the Institute building was from the 1990s, before the railings around the forecourt walls had been reinstated.

There were images in this pop-up exhibition that showed how the interior of the building had changed, including one of the detail of the bar counter in the Hackworth Lounge; its panels showing the development of the railway locomotive throughout the years. The first of these depicted "Stephenson's Locomotion No. 1," followed in sequence by "Rocket," Hackworth's "Royal George" and "Derwent," "Patentee," Tennent's 2-4-0, Sir Nigel Gresley's "Silver Link" locomotive, and a diesel Deltic.

Other photographs depicted scenes from various events at the Institute. Among these, the visit of the last Railway Queen in 1974, several depicting prize-giving at the annual horticultural show and others showing buffets, bazaars and beautiful displays of home grown produce.

Also displayed in this exhibition were blown-up copies of selected pages from the Centenary Book telling the story of the building's opening back in 1913, so that visitors could imagine the events of that day.

Overall the display was a delightful retrospective, and opportunity to take stock of the Institute's time in residence at Redworth Road. Members could take time to admire the images and seek out family members from among the faces on display. In addition a paper banner was purchased to display on the high ceiling above the stage in the main hall, declaring the building's centenary. It remained there until it was removed in 2022.

"Save Our Stute"

After the annual accounts had been prepared for the financial year up to the end of December 2018, there was concern circulating through the members of the committee. The financial reserves of the Institute were perilously low, and the Institute was losing around £1000 per month. The situation had become precarious to the point where rumours abounded that the 2019 Annual General Meeting would include an announcement that the Institute would be certain to close for good that year.

This news reached Fred Langley, a retired tutor who had not long returned to Shildon after a long career teaching young theatre performers around the world. Fred's brother, Kenny Langley was a loyal regular member at the Institute, and their father had once served as Treasurer on the Committee. Fred was mortified at the prospect of this long standing legacy for Shildon being lost, so reached out to a Town Councillor, Dave Reynolds, also an Institute member, with whom he had recently discussed views on the depreciated state of the town as a whole.

Reynolds, based on his brief experiences as a Councillor, felt that there would be no quick fixes available through the political process. The Town Council, running on a tight budget, was limited to offering only community grants of maximum fifty pounds value, and did not have a fund to help with this type of situation. When consulted, fellow Town Councillors felt that it was just a sign of the times that the Institute had fallen on hardship, that it was just one of many problems in the town and not a priority. Reynolds felt differently, and carried a hope that that if the community rallied to pull together, the decline at the Institute could be reversed, albeit gradually, to a point where it could become stable and viable again. He also felt it would require a new and different community organisation to try to lead that charge. Failure was always possible, but given the Institute's unique heritage it would be worth trying.

The result was that a small movement of people, beginning with Dave and Fred, assembled with to trying to help out. A meeting took place between that group and the Institute's Committee, and an offer to help was expressed and agreed.

The new group's first objective was to find out whether there was sufficient weight of support upon which the Institute might build a survival campaign. A proposal agreed by the group was to invite members and community to a public meeting to discuss the predicament. The consequent meeting took place on the evening of Wednesday 22 May 2019. Posters were liberally displayed in advance, and hand flyers delivered to every door in the New Shildon neighbourhood.

When the meeting day came, the main hall at the Institute was packed with members and interested members of the public. Institute secretary Shaun Thompson addressed the assembly setting out the financial situation, followed by Dave Reynolds, who set out his opinion that the Institute's unique place as a world first in the region's railway story made a great case for fighting for its survival. He said he believed that an ambitious plan should be set out, not only to revitalise the Institute but to seek significant refurbishment before the Public Steam Passenger Railway Bicentenary Celebrations took place in 2025. A whole range of views and opinions were offered on what should happen, and volunteers took notes on the sidelines. The campaigners promised to provide a suggestion box for members to capture their feedback, and that the new volunteer group and committee would act on as much of this as possible.

The wave of public support, and demonstration of a resolve to fight on, proved heartening and convinced the small volunteer group that a "Save Our Stute" campaign with a stated goal of reversing the decline in the Institute's fortunes was a viable option. Fred Langley, Dave Reynolds, Kelly Ambrosini and Sue Clarke set up a separate small Community Interest Company, or CIC, called the Shildon Heritage Alliance, that would, among other things, work alongside the Institute Committee. In time others joined this movement, each bringing different skills and a willingness to work together as volunteers. Establishing this company as a second independent organisation was intended to protect the Institute from any unwanted direct controlling influence of the campaign group. This was thought to be a good compromise given that many long standing Institute members were initially suspicious of the group's motives for helping. It also enabled the CIC to progress other non-Institute related heritage projects.

The campaign group immersed itself in the process of trying to understand the strengths and weaknesses of how the Institute operated, as well as raising its profile within the community and beyond. They also set about organising a programme of events that would bring new people into the Institute, boost membership, and put the building back on the map as a venue and destination. Efforts were made to try to meet any realistic suggestions put forward by members. The new group also set out to research and promote the rich cultural heritage of the Institute, reconnecting members with that story. Further efforts were made to build new relationships and partnerships with other organisations in the area.

Some parts of the building still in regular use had become shabby and looked uncared for, through a general state of disrepair. Funds, raised through ticketed events, were used to give these a 'spruce-up' in an attempt to make the Institute more enjoyable to visit and use again. Much of this was achieved through the help of volunteers, from the membership, from the campaign, or from local businesses such as the Shildon site of the PPG paint company. Slowly but surely the Institute began to take on a new life, and membership also began to swell once more.

Sadly, the turnaround in fortunes did not come quickly enough to give Shildon Amateur Boxing Club confidence not to leave their base of operations on the first floor of the Institute. They had, quite naturally, been concerned about the impact that possible closure of the Institute would have on their operation. Would they, yet again, be left them without a home? Boxing club officials took the difficult decision to look for a new building in which to host their training facilities.

After initially looking to rent a property from Durham County Council, which proved unaffordable, the club eventually struck a deal with Old Shildon Club, to use their upper floor. The departure of the boxing club meant that the whole of the Institute's first floor was vacant once more, and in very poor condition.

Those first six months of the Save Our Stute campaign saw a flurry of local community fundraising activity that contributed to the costs of a range of small but high priority changes. These included essential temporary roof repairs, a building condition survey, purchase of card payment equipment, solicitor's fees relating to the appointment of new Trustees to replace those that had passed away, modifications to club rules to formally allow non British Rail employees to become members and some essential ground maintenance. An ambitious outline plan was drawn up to try to navigate a course to further major goals and a fully revived Institute by September 2025.

Making an Exhibition of Ourselves

One of the objectives set by the Shildon Heritage Alliance, when entering its partnership with the Institute, was to reconnect the organisation with what makes it culturally unique.

In most ways Shildon ceased to be a railway town when its works closed in 1984, though it still remained connected to the nation's rail network. If asked, many would say that they have 'moved on' from thinking of it as a railway town. Perhaps in part it's because they feel they have had to do so. The works, jobs, wealth and wellbeing that the industry brought, would never return. In the forty years since closure nothing on a comparable scale has stepped in to fill the void. What is the sense of causing yourself hurt by dwelling on the matter?

But there are also still many folk who, if they pause for long enough, can bring to mind the echo of the relentless ring of the enormous drop hammers at the works forge, or the sight and sound of a train of newly fabricated or freshly repaired wagons rolling out over the Mason's Arms railway crossing and off through the southern quarter of town en route to far-flung places around the world. There are still a good many older men who remember the camaraderie, characters, humour and sense of shared purpose that bound the Shildon workforce together, and who if asked will tell you that they would go back to it in a heartbeat despite so many having now passed retirement age. There is still a tremendous romance associated with the railways. It still attracts a broad inter-generational fascination. You just need to look to some of the small towns connected to the key heritage railways of Britain to see that. Pickering on the North Yorkshire Moors Railway. Bewdley and Bridgenorth on the Severn Valley Railway. What is stopping Shildon from using its past to imagine becoming a 'destination town' with a brighter, albeit different, future?

2019 brought an appropriate opportunity to bring a cluster of those surviving engineering men from the former Shildon workforce together to share reminiscences and tell tales, with pride and great mischief in equal measure. The volunteers and committee at the Institute put their heads together to arrange a reunion to mark the thirty-five years since the closure of Shildon Works.

The Shildon Heritage Alliance, hoping to create something unique in honour of the occasion, set about planning an exhibition about the works, along with a documentary video that would premiere on the day. The latter was an oral reflection on life at Shildon Works as seen through the eyes of several of the last intake of engineering apprentices. The project also included interviews with one or two older retired employees. The stories were woven together with images of the works throughout the years, along with some specially commissioned stunning aerial footage showing the former works site in the present. The whole thing was shot, edited and produced by the SHA volunteers, with the interviews themselves being recorded in the Institute's main hall. Upon completion, the documentary movie, running at over an hour in length, was given the title "The Full Works".

This reunion took place on Saturday 5 October 2019. Former employees, some of whom had travelled some distance to return to a town they had left decades ago, arrived at the Institute main hall to find the walls had been decorated with huge vinyl banners featuring blown up images of the men at work, crowded together leaving the works at end of shift, or gathered together to hear the speeches made during the campaign to keep it open. Some had brought their families, including younger members who had never seen what life at the works would have been like. Tables had been laid out with identification plates from the various different wagons that the works had produced, photographs and other memories. A special display had been prepared by Alan Ellwood of the Shildon History Recall Society, whose enormous archive contained artefacts, papers and photographs illustrating daily life at the works. The Shildon Works No. 2 Branch National Union of Railwaymen banner, made in Shildon in the 1970s, was placed back on display for the first time in many decades, having been graciously returned to the community and Institute by the Auckland Railways Group, its most recent in a line of custodians.

Above: Former BREL Shildon Works employees and their families begin to arrive at the 2019 Institute exhibition held to mark the 35th anniversary of the closure of the works.

After the doors were opened, the hall gradually filled up with former Shildon Works employees, some of whom had brought along families to meet their old comrades. The atmosphere inside the hall was charged with chattering, punctuated by outbreaks of laughter, triggered by fond and humorous memories. On a large screen a series of films were projected, including "The Full Works", a compilation of news footage covering the closure of the works, a television documentary brought by the Stabler family telling of the impact of the closure of the works, and vintage cine footage taken of the town during the 150th Stockton & Darlington Railway celebrations in 1975.

MARKING 4 YEARS TO THE UPCOMING STEAM PASSENGER RAILWAY BICENTENARY

RAIL STORIES TOLD BY LOCAL SOCIETIES THROUGH IMAGES OBJECTS SOUNDS WORDS AND FILM

MASONS ARMS CROSSING SLEEPER INSTALLATION WILL BE DEDICATED AT 10:00 AM

EXHIBITION THEN OPEN FROM NOON ONWARDS

5 SEPTEMBER 2021

SHILDON RAILWAY INSTITUTE

www.shildonrailway.institute/whatson/exhibition2021

Above: Poster design for the 2021 Annual Rail Heritage Exhibition at the Institute which was inspired by the success of the 2019 Works Reunion. It had been postponed from 2020 due to the Covid outbreak.

The 2019 works reunion event proved such a success that it spawned the idea of an annual Rail Heritage Exhibition, co-ordinated by volunteer John Raw, and showcasing the town and area's industrial culture and place in the region's railway story. By coincidence, in the following year, 2020, the annual anniversary of the opening of the Stockton & Darlington Railway, which took place on 27 September, would fall on a Saturday, so it was planned that this first general Rail Heritage Exhibition at the Institute would take place on that date.

Yet even as that plan was being conceived, there was a sudden new and highly dramatic turn of events that heralded a new threat to this venerable but vulnerable community institution.

Pandemic

In December of 2019, reports began to circulate in the news of cases of a worrying new life-threatening virus with no known effective treatment. The first reports were centred upon the city of Wuhan in China, which seemed so far away from Shildon. Within a few weeks, British TV news channels and newspapers were showing images of coach loads of British passengers returning from China and being escorted by police from Heathrow Airport. Cases of the new illness soon began to be reported, with increasing frequency, within the United Kingdom, and by 11 March the medical situation was beginning to be referred to as a pandemic. The virus became known as Covid-19, and a widespread panic ensued. By 18 March the UK Government were advocating social distancing, avoidance of non-essential travel and working from home. Everyone had an opinion on the new illness, and differing views on the necessity for precautionary measures divided people almost as bitterly as the Brexit debate had four years previous. On 20 March the Prime Minister ordered that all social, hospitality and leisure businesses close with immediate effect. This was the beginning of a year long period in which the Institute was at various points either fully closed, operating restricted hours or else under very restricted operating practices.

Whether the Institute was closed, or even trading at well below its optimal levels, bills were still coming in and still had to be paid. During that winter the Institute building was also subjected to damage from heavy snowfall and leaks from melt water, which required critical repairs. Large quantities of drink stock became unsellable, could not be returned, and had to be written off.

Across the nation, individuals continued to argue over whether these 'lockdowns' were justified or not, given the threat to jobs and businesses. Some felt we should be allowed to decide for ourselves and take our chances. Others on the fringes argued that there was no pandemic and that the whole situation was a fabricated shadowy international conspiracy. Nonetheless the rules were strictly enforced and had to be adhered to. Local authorities and police monitored hospitality venues and social buildings, including the Institute, ensuring that they remained closed. Hefty fines were issued to organisations that breached the new restrictions.

The Government quickly realised that, in order to avoid an intolerable long term burden on the benefit system from workers losing their jobs, it made fiscal sense to protect those jobs by offering a less expensive temporary furlough scheme. This enabled hospitality staff to remain in-post, on standby, able to return straight to their jobs when the restrictions lifted. This in turn meant that the Institute Committee were able to retain the Stewardess and other staff. In the meantime, volunteers and Committee worked together to make sure that the Institute was equipped with obligatory safety signage, protective equipment, cleaning materials and other measures so that, when they became able to trade again, as normal a service as possible could be offered to the members. A rota system was drawn up, ensuring that when the building was allowed to open there were volunteers on hand to take names and contact details for the mandatory Government Track and Trace scheme. Volunteers and staff cleaned toilets, tables and other surfaces at hourly intervals. Everyone worked together like a well oiled machine to try to help the Institute survive through this almost indeterminable dark spell.

During the period in the warmer summer months of 2020, when national restrictions were briefly relaxed, the Institute building re-opened for business. Trading was still subject to considerable restrictions and public booking of the facilities was still prohibited. Reduced opening hours were imposed and table service for drinks was mandated. Visitors entered and left the building via a strict one-way system. Plastic screens were erected to protect the bar staff from coughs and vapours, with staff wearing protective visors as they served at tables. Those that visited the Institute were permitted to sit only with other members of their 'household bubble' and had to wear a face mask when not seated to prevent spreading the disease. Singing or dancing of any description were prohibited, making it a joyless time for the members. Nonetheless, while they were able to, many were keen to visit and spend time together, albeit in a socially distanced manner. Doing so was a welcome relief from the isolation of life under the threat of Covid.

On 18 October 2020, just a couple of weeks before the national instruction came to 'lock-down' once again for the winter months, the Institute even managed to hold a single compliant and socially distanced concert for members, featuring the popular sixties band The Fabs. Even though the main hall was sparsely populated with small household groups sat at spaced out tables, unable to dance or sing along, it was a rare night of relief and a moment of near normality. By early November everyone was once again ordered to stay at home, and like other hospitality venues the

Institute once again closed for business.

Above: The Institute's only concert event held during the Covid 19 pandemic, conducted in a compliant and socially distanced manner on 18 October 2020 and featuring The Fabs.

A relief scheme was introduced to help businesses and organisations with a percentage of their running costs while they were forced to close. During the periods when it was permitted to be open, the Institute's ability to make money was still significantly restricted, for example by imposed shorter hours, and the Institute once again came perilously close to financial failure.

In early November of 2020, specifically the couple of weeks leading up to what would have been the Institute's 187th anniversary date, an idea emerged to broadcast an online birthday party concert over the internet. This would be something that people across the town, and perhaps further afield, could enjoy at home, but which, when combined with an appeal, also might raise some money to help the Institute pay bills during this difficult period. A number of local music artists, some of whom were Institute members, were approached with a request to make a video of themselves performing a song at home to be compiled into the show. Many responded with generosity, including Richie Boddy,

Bosko Green, Steve and Jayne Todd, Ruth Stapleton, Citizen Songwriters, Brian Heslop, Samantha Mac, Darren Johnson, Glenn Maltman, Phil Graham and Irish folk band Share the Darkness. With these contributions, the online concert lasted over an hour and was watched by over 600 households on the night.

This show was scheduled to coincide with the start of a crowd-funding campaign, collecting donations through payments made using an online payment solution. Some additional applications were raised for Covid resilience funding grants, and overall these efforts managed to realise a total return of £16,000. This generous support from the community played a huge part in the Institute surviving the Covid crisis.

It was a remarkable show of support, with the whole community collaborating to show their love and respect for the troubled community organisation. As with the popular saying about a cat having nine lives, it seemed as though the Institute had expended another of its lives, and lived on to tell the tale.

There was a great deal of relief when announcements began to be made that a first Covid vaccine had been developed, bringing hope that the devastating virus which had been such a threat could be mitigated. In the grand scheme of things, the Institute's struggle for survival paled into insignificance alongside the dangers faced by key workers during the crisis, those on the front line who had risked contracting the virus to help us all day-to-day, or the families that had lost loved ones to the illness. Yet it was still such a relief when the summer of 2021 brought steps back toward resuming normal operation at the Institute. It would not to be a return to full normality. Some who had been regular visitors pre-pandemic no longer felt it safe to come out again to socialise in numbers.

Socially, financially and operationally the pandemic was such a set back that it had become clear that a five year plan would no longer be realistic, and that the group needed to plan ten years ahead, looking to the Institute's own bicentenary in 2033 as a new target for a full revival plan.

Come Sing With Us

Emerging from the viral pandemic it was clear that in many respects the world had changed socially and behaviourally. Many had become more accustomed to 'staying in' rather than going out to meet people socially. For some this suited them perfectly. For others it left them feeling lonely and isolated; particularly those with health worries or who hadn't many family members to rely upon during the crisis. As the first and most serious wave of the pandemic eased, there was also a sense that some people might find it difficult to return to socialising again.

At the Institute there was a feeling that it would be helpful to put on an activity to encourage isolated folk to come out and spend time together, in a space large enough for people to separate themselves appropriately whilst still doing something together.

Taking inspiration from the kinds of societies that had been connected to the Institute in the past, a popular idea was to create a socially distanced community singing group that could be enjoyed by anyone, and that could be joined on a donations only subscription basis so that nobody would feel excluded through affordability. One of the first groups to have benefitted from the Institute's first hall in 1860 had been a choral society. A revival of singing together could well be the perfect tonic to the new twenty-first century problem.

The Shildon Heritage Alliance worked with the Institute to initiate the project, and made contact with a friendly local singing coach with experience of community singing groups. This was Rosie Bradford, a self employed music teacher trading under the name of Happy in Harmony Music. Rosie had been involved in a project run with Opera North and Northern Heartlands, which had centred on Shildon as a focal point and which had been called "Song of Our Heartland". That project had created a full length community opera involving professional and amateur singers, some of whom were from Shildon. The culmination of the project had been a video recording of the opera on location at the Locomotion museum. Rosie's combination of proficiency and relaxed informal friendly nature made her a perfect choice to coach the new community singing group.

At the time the idea arose, the country was still subject to social restrictions including a ban on singing indoors; but a few outdoor meetings with Rosie led to plans that could be executed when the warmer months returned. By that time the numbers of virus cases was expected to reduce and restrictions to be relaxed. Singing sessions were hoped to be scheduled for early Friday evenings, to enable people to join after work but not so late that they would interfere with other Friday evening plans.

A first 'meet and greet' session, to which people could come to meet Rosie, was arranged for Friday 21 May 2021, and an announcement was published in the Shildon Town Crier declaring the new singing group. Posters were put out in prominent places around the town, and fliers were posted through letterboxes throughout the streets.

By July the Shildon Institute Singers were off to a good start, with an inclusive approach that didn't require anyone to read music, also allowing the group to suggest which songs they would like to try. The spacious hall gave everyone enough room to socially distance as they sang a combination of rock and pop hits along with songs from musicals that people enjoyed. It was an eclectic mix, and not always to the taste of everyone who attended. Some came along hoping for a more formal approach, and decided that the relaxed sessions weren't for them. Most of the folk who attended enjoyed the informal 'come as you please' approach and formed a loyal and friendly core at the heart of the new singing group.

Above: Rosie Bradford (far right) puts a group of Shildon Institute Singers through their paces at a rehearsal.

Relaxed and inclusive as the Shildon Institute Singers were, they still found ways to involve members in opportunities to perform publicly. The Institute held its Rail Heritage Exhibition, involving rail history interest groups from Witton park to Stockton all exhibiting their collections, at which the Singers took to the stage. The group also offered a programme of wartime singalong songs at a fundraising concert to help Alan Ellwood of the Shildon History Recall Society to pay for a bronze plaque to commemorate the crew of a crashed Stirling bomber that had come down on the outskirts of Shildon during the Second World War. The singing group also gave Christmas concerts for the Butterwick Hospice and on the platform of Stanhope Station as part of a Story Train event there. Their most exciting opportunity was to be invited to participate in a recording project, for which the seeds had been sown several months before the singing group started.

In June of 2020, Sam Slatcher, a director of Durham based Citizen Songwriters, reached out to the Shildon Heritage Alliance volunteers at the Institute with an opportunity to collaborate on a digital storytelling project. The project was to be entitled "Life Along the Line" and intended to create songs based upon the lived experiences and thoughts of people who reside in communities along the route of the former Stockton and Darlington Railway. The Institute became one of a number of agreeable partners collaborating on the project. Sam submitted an application for necessary funding required to bring the project to life.

Word of success on the funding bid didn't return until early January 2021, at which time Britain was still in that state of 'lockdown' due to the Covid-19 pandemic. The funding body appreciated that Citizen Songwriters had taken precautions in the project plan by making provision for several of the sessions to take place outdoors, virtually over a video communications platform called Zoom that became popular during the pandemic, or in large socially distanced spaces like the main hall at the Institute.

The first workshop featured, among other things, a historical lecture by Niall Hammond, of the Friends of the Stockton and Darlington Railway, and reminiscences of life at Shildon Works, and took place using Zoom on 28 April 2021. A guided walk, taking in some of Shildon's most notable railway heritage, took place on 1 June, and further face to face discussion group sessions took place on Tuesday 1 and Friday 11 June. During these, people shared their own stories, recollections and suggestions as contributions toward the co-creation of the new songs. Attendance to these workshops was free of charge, but attendees were given an optional opportunity to contribute a donation to help the Institute.

A further concert session, showing off some of the resulting songs, took place at the Locomotion Museum in Shildon on Thursday 15 July, to which the town's schools were invited to attend and participate. The concert was only 30 minutes in duration, and commenced with the passing of the 13:14pm train on the Bishop Line, which featured in the children's own song that opened the concert. The concert event concluded the project, or so everyone thought at the time.

On 17 September, Sam Slatcher got back in touch again to say that he had learned that Durham County Council had additional funding available for community cultural events, and that he was thinking of applying to run another project to build upon the success of the Life Along the Line project in Shildon. This time Sam's idea was to create more songs and to conclude the venture by capturing them for posterity in a recording session. His idea was to create a temporary recording studio at the Institute.

By then the Shildon Institute Singers were fully up and running, so Sam made sure that the little community singing group were firmly part of the plan, engaging Rosie Bradford as choir co-ordinator. On 8 October, he contacted everyone again to let them know that his follow-up funding application, based on feedback from the first project as part of its justification, had been a success, and that the workshops and recording session would go ahead before the spring.

Above: One section of the Shildon Institute Singers in the main hall during recording of tracks for the Citizen Songwriters "Songs of Shildon" project.

Following a recommendation, Sam engaged sound technology and recording company Xtrasonic Media, who were based at Cockfield, not far from Shildon, and plans were drawn up relating to how the project might run. In the meantime, Rosie and the Shildon Institute Singers began to include some of the songs from the Citizen Songwriters project into their singing sessions. Once again a newly evolved and menacing variant of the Covid virus, named the 'Omicron' variant, had begin to spread through the population, and the return of wintry conditions had driven everyone back indoors speeding up the transition rate. Consequently attendance numbers at the singing sessions had dipped a little but, confident that precautions were being followed, the singing continued. In addition Sam and Rosie commenced reaching out to a few local musicians, including classically trained violinist Cathy Edmunds who had become well known in part through her work with Irish band Share The Darkness, and who was by then putting together a new folk-rock band. Sam's aim was to create an overall sound based upon the area's talent. He planned to have a rehearsal day on Saturday 22 January 2022, with recording days following soon after on 27 and 28 January and a "Cradle of the Railways" concert event on April 1 at which the new songs would be performed live onstage in the Institute main hall.

There was a little rehearsal time available for the participating musicians, which included Sam himself, as well as Citizen Songwriters co-Director Alex Summerson, to work through their musical contributions. Then it was time to record.

Graham Kay, owning Director of Xtrasonic Media, arrived at the Institute for the recording weekend, bringing with him an array of high-tech portable recording equipment. He set about the task of converting the Institute Hall into a suitable recording environment, which given the natural creaks and quirks of the hall proved an interesting challenge. Participants removed their shoes so as to create as little noise as possible on the hall's sprung dance floor. Throughout the recording you can hear occasional noises created by the general ambience of the building, a creak of the floor or metallic rattle from the hundred-and-ten-year-old natural ventilation system.

The instrumental recordings were laid down first, so that the singers would be able to hear their accompaniment, then the task of recording the voices followed. Given that the Shildon Institute Singers were recording for the first time, Alex Summerson walked the slightly nervous group through their parts with a calm experienced manner. The group were broken into three singing sections that would each be recoded separately.

Though the project had quite a few songs under its belt, the constraint of time led to the musicians and singers recording only five of them. These were "Shildon Town", a sing-along anthem relating the friendliness, geographical location and ambience of Shildon as a community, a song which involved the choir, "Wonderful Giants of Old," a storytelling of the first five miles of the Stockton and Darlington Railway, "Footsteps of Giants," an atmospheric piece on ancestry featuring singing coach Rosie Bradford on vocal as well as some impressive jazz trumpet from a young James Goldberg, a pupil of Rosie. There were two other songs, a storytelling piece, "Set The World On Track," which included the reminiscences of people travelling on the Bishop Line captured during the year the project was run, and an acapella cover of Bill Withers's classic hit "Lean on Me", which had become a favourite of the choir and which they felt summed up the spirit of the town.

Above: Xtrasonic Media's engineer, Graham Kay, temporarily converted the Institute's main hall to a recording studio on two occasions.

With the recording work complete rehearsals continued in a build up to the April 1 concert which featured the same songs, with one or two of the ones that had not been able to be included in the recording session. The concert performance was an intimate rendition, being mainly acoustic instruments and voices, but was enjoyed by a still reasonable number of people despite worries over transference of the Covid virus leading to fewer people attending than hoped. The project had still been deemed very successful in achieving its aims, and there were other opportunities throughout that year at which the songs could be heard.

Citizen Songwriters produced one thousand copies of a CD of the recordings entitled "Cradle of the Railways" which was officially released on 15 July 2022, with the recordings being added to streaming platforms at the same time.

One final side-project from the original Songs of Shildon project was initiated later that year, centring again on the activities of the Shildon Institute Singers. This involved one of the songs that hadn't been selected for the CD recording, and which had been created by Dave Reynolds of the Shildon Heritage Alliance CIC who was also part of the choir. The song was "The Light at the End of the Shildon Tunnel," which had been prompted by an observation, by John Raw of the Brusselton Incline Group, that 2022 marked the 120th anniversary of the opening of the Prince of Wales Tunnel beneath the town of Shildon.

We already explained early in this book that it was the opening of this tunnel in 1842 that created the opportunity for the Institute to have its first reading room, and that this was the first passenger railway tunnel in the world to pass beneath a town. It seemed appropriate for the singing group to mark that occasion. Despite the historic connection the song was forward looking, with lyrics expressing hope for a brighter future for the town's people.

A small grant of £1,000 was successfully secured from Create North to cover the cost of singing tuition and recording. Planning began at the end of July 2022, with Xtrasonic Media's Graham Kay booked to record the new song again in the Institute main hall. Meanwhile Dave also arranged the song for three harmonising parts; alto, soprano and tenor. This was the most ambitious arrangement the choir had attempted to date, so tutor Rosie Bradford coached the Shildon Institute Singers through their parts at their Friday evening rehearsal sessions.

This time, rather than producing a CD, the recorded song was accompanied by a video, so the singers were asked to contribute ideas of their favourite views of their hometown which would be included as scenes in the video. The recording session took place on 2 October, requiring the main hall at the Institute to once again serve as a makeshift recording studio.

Following a brief window of opportunity to edit the music and video footage together, an in-person premiere screening event, featuring a concert by Shildon Institute Singers took place on 14 October, followed by an online release of the video and song as a tribute to the tunnel on 17 October.

The Shildon Institute Singers continued until June of 2023, by which point its coach, Rosie, had encountered some medical issues making it difficult for her to commit to regular weekly sessions. The group had already planned to take a break during the summer months when Rosie, and many members, took holidays, but entered something of an extended hiatus. There are hopes of more Shildon Institute Singers activities in the future.

Iconic Shildon Banners Return

In 2022 one of Shildon's most important and symbolic industrial cultural objects returned to permanent display for the first time in decades, and the Institute was its destination.

The artefact in question was a silk trade union banner,

created in 1919, that had been for some years in the possession of the Auckland Railways Group. That group had been keen to see the banner return to Shildon, and for it to be put on display rather than hidden away. To mark its return, along with that of a much younger trade union banner from the 1970s, the SHA organised a grand unveiling event which featured some of the Songs of Shildon written in the community as part of the Citizen Songwriters project the previous year.

As the banner was originally created for, and paid for by, members of, the National Union of Railwaymen in Shildon, and that this particular trade union had later been absorbed into the Rail, Maritime and Transport Workers Union (RMT), the organisers invited the serving RMT General Secretary, Michael Lynch, to speak and unveil the banner. This was doubly appropriate as the RMT had not only contributed to the Auckland Railways Group's efforts to repair the banner, but also to the Institute's own fundraising campaigns.

Another key speaker at the unveiling event was Gerald Slack of the Auckland Railways Group who spoke of his group's acquisition of the banner, and difficulties but determination in getting it repaired. He also explained the appropriateness of it being displayed at the Institute. He was followed by Shaun Thompson, at that time the Secretary of the Railway Institute, who presented Mr Lynch with an honorary lifetime membership of the Institute.

The huge banner, around ten feet square, had been manufactured in 1919 for the National Union of Railwaymen Shildon Works No. 2 Branch. It depicts the Shildon Works at its industrial peak viewed from the eastern end near the Masons Arms railway crossing. For some reason it had been put in unprotected storage in an attic decades earlier, which along with the passage of time had led to its fabric becoming very fragile. Gerald and his colleague, Michael O'Neill, also of the Auckland Railways Group, had patiently raised money to have the banner carefully repaired by a leading restorer. They had been advised against full restoration on the grounds that the banner would lose much of its authentic and historical quality. The Shildon Heritage Alliance CIC, through its own event based fundraising, paid for the timber and polycarbonate used in the construction of the new purpose built case, which was designed and built by Institute Committee member Selwyn Jenkin. Speaking of his motivation for repairing it, Gerald said:

"When we were granted custodianship of it in 2016, by the National Railway Museum, we were saddened by its poor condition as a consequence of unfavourable storage and the ravages of time, and acutely aware of the imperative to restore it to save it for posterity and display it in the town. There was also a personal interest in restoring and displaying the banner as both my grandfather and great-grandfather worked at Shildon Works, as did many members of my wife's family."

It is thought to be one of the earliest surviving NUR banners, having been commissioned only six years after the union's founding. Given the delicacy of its silk damask fabric its survival is in itself an achievement. It was made by George Tutill and Co., a London company founded in 1837 and the best known of the banner makers in Britain at the time. They were tremendously expensive, so seen as symbolic of the power and success of each union branch. On its new home, Mr Slack told those present,

"Shildon Railway Institute is absolutely the right place to display the banner. Standing close to the Shildon Works site, its own history is entirely synonymous with the legacy of the works. We remain ever grateful to the RMT for kick starting the appeal. Also to the local people and enterprises that contributed to the appeal, and the unstinting support of Shildon Football Club, the Town Crier and Mike Amos."

The further coincidental connection between banner and host building is that the NUR was formed just less than two months after the current Shildon Railway Institute building was opened for use. The banner was visited briefly on unveiling day by some younger relatives, as an act of tribute. The Newcastle Rail and Catering Branch, and the Newcastle and Gateshead Branch, of the RMT brought along their current banners, which depict hand-painted scenes of iconic bridges and rail architecture and engineering on Tyneside. The 1970s Shildon Works No.2 branch banner was also present and on display for the occasion. It is hoped that this too might be put on permanent display at the Institute.

Mr Lynch, during his speech, which included well researched factual detail of the development of the town's trade union branches, also presented the Institute with two fine gifts. The first was a banner bearer's sash, once worn by a members of a team carrying a banner or supporting ropes at a demonstration. This was from the era before the founding of the National Union of Railwaymen, and it bears the initials of the forerunning Amalgamated Society of Railway Servants (ASRS) which later became part of the NUR. That fact is acknowledged on the 1919 banner. The second item was a framed NUR Centenary Certificate dedicated to the Shildon Works No.2 Branch. Both items were since put on display at the Institute in the MacNay Room.

Above: RMT General Secretary, Mick Lynch, presents the Institute with an ASRS banner carrier's sash at the unveiling of the 1919 National Union of Railwaymen Shildon Works Number 2 Branch banner.

Institute Secretary, Shaun Thompson expressed appreciation on behalf of the Institute, particularly to Mr Jenkin for his part in creating the case to enable the banner's return, as well as fellow Committee member, Adam Thompson for assisting Mr Jenkin. Other statements of appreciation were also shared.

The banner was unveiled at 1:30pm on 5 Feb 2022 in the tightly packed entrance hall of the Institute. A red satin cover, was removed on cue by Mr Lynch and Anthony Knight, of the SHA, who had assisted in the fitting and cosmetic completion of the display case. The sight of the historic banner being revealed was met with applause and expressions of enjoyment. This moment served as an important step forward in reconnecting the Institute and community of Shildon with more of its unique cultural and industrial heritage.

Above: Shildon Railway Institute Secretary, Shaun Thompson, addresses members and visitors at the unveiling of the banner which was arranged through the kind cooperation of the Auckland Railways Group.

The Library is Reborn

2022 brought a further, perhaps surprising, opportunity to reflect the Institute's historic role in the town. From its very inception the Institute had been centred upon the notion of providing knowledge through what became a very extensive and informative library of books. As we explained, the collection had been a combination of literary classics, instructional publications on moral and technical matters, and works on history, travel and practical engineering.

As the second half of the twentieth-century wore on however, interest in this once staple offering was dwindling. This could have been for a number of reasons. Books had certainly become more commonplace possessions of the working classes and were easily accessible elsewhere. Additionally, the membership of the Institute had expanded considerably in its new premises, and those members had more say in the priorities of the organisation. Promotion of more fun and sociable pastimes overtook the interest in sharing knowledge. The Institute had been founded and governed for many decades by men who wanted 'good things' for the working people of Shildon. A sense of improved prospects, and certainly a more responsible and educated workforce. The situation had now evolved to a point where the members wanted a committee that would steer things in directions they preferred.

In considering the story of the Institute from its beginning, I've hypothesised that had George Graham, Thomas MacNay and Timothy Hackworth met with the men that had been placing bets on those frying pocket watches at the Globe Inn back in 1833, and asked them what they would want in order to be more contented, they might well have received the response "More pocket watches to fry!" I write that in jest, but what I mean is that sometimes you might lose sight of potentially valuable or useful opportunity, to focus instead on something more novel and fun.

Thus it was that, at some point after 1960, a decision was made to dispose of the Institute's original, and quite extensive, library collection. Had it been retained, or even placed out of the way in storage, it might now have been a very valuable collection both monetarily and culturally. If you've ever visited an antiquarian bookshop and browsed the shelves then you'll have an idea of what a large collection stretching back to the early nineteenth century might be worth today. What actually happened to the books is really quite obscure, though some volumes at least, identifiable by the 'Shildon LNER Institute' markings on their spines, or embossing on internal pages, did make their way into the private collections of former members.

Nowadays, for so many people, the idea of visiting a library to learn about a topic, is considered an old-fashioned and inefficient way to acquire knowledge and understanding. It's generally more convenient to bring up an internet search engine on an electronic device close to hand and run a cursory search on a subject. You'll certainly find a great deal of information that way; some of it produced by reputable sources, some of it less so. But will you find everything you wanted to know, or that is there to be known? There is still a huge amount of knowledge and reference material that does not yet exist in the digital realm, and will likely never be placed there in our lifetime. Might there still be a place for a library in the digital information era?

That question was exactly what was on the mind of the Institute's volunteers when they were considering what to do with one of the disused rooms on the first floor of the Institute building that had been vacated by Shildon Amateur Boxing Club when they moved out in 2019. It was left in pretty poor condition; not specifically as a consequence of the Boxing Club's occupation, rather through decades of neglect. But one feature that remained was a fixed wall unit with a series of five tall two-tier cupboards. It was felt that these could easily be adapted to create bookshelves. These in turn might be used to display some of the artefacts that the Institute had retained, as well as a small collection of books that volunteers already held or that had been donated by Institute well-wishers. There wasn't much, but this change could be made as part of a spruce-up to bring the room back to some useful purpose as a meeting room for clubs and societies.

Above: A party of volunteers from BT's Business Design team set about the first phase of sprucing up and painting a disused room on the Institute's first floor.

The idea wasn't so much to re-introduce a broad library covering all subjects as a very focused library covering only two subjects. Insight into, the railway industry, with as much emphasis as possible on our town, and region's part in that story, and material specific to the people of Shildon, the surrounding towns and villages and our unique industrial culture.

With this goal in mind, volunteers set about making the

room more comfortable. A plan was set out to redecorate it using a traditional palette. Three colour schemes were shared, with a view to canvassing opinions on which would be the best. The first was a 'blood and custard' paint scheme based upon the British Rail combination of 'crimson lake' and 'cream' as once used on railway coaches. The second was a pale blue and cream scheme based upon the livery of the Deltic locomotive. The winning scheme was inspired by the green, black and cream livery of the North Eastern Railway Company's locomotives and stock.

A volunteering session, involving a party of BT employees, set out to execute the first wave of cosmetic work. Subsequent fundraising enabled the acquisition of a new carpet, while a volunteer offered to donate new tables for the room. The door to this room had previously been removed by the Boxing Club to enable free movement of the young boxers around the first floor. This was located, repainted and replaced. Light fittings were donated by local businessman, Paul Harle, who also arranged fitting of the carpets and replacement of broken window panes.

It was at this point that a chance fortuitous opportunity arose. Shildon Heritage Alliance volunteer, Anthony Knight, spotted that the nearby group, the Friends of the Darlington Railway Museum, were looking to sell, or find a new home for, a large collection of railway books that they had been maintaining at Darlington's Head of Steam Museum. That museum, which had, in a small but important way, been supported financially by the Friends for many decades, was about to undergo a significant physical redevelopment. After this, there would be no place at the museum for their book collection of around six hundred railway books. The Institute and the Friends of the Darlington Railway Museum had matching needs at just the right time.

Anthony set up a meeting with John Lawrie of the Friends group, who offered a tour of their collection. Subsequent discussions within the two separate committees led to a subsequent agreement between Institute, Friends and the Shildon Heritage Alliance. The latter organisation would become custodians of the book collection at the Institute.

A final point of negotiation was the naming of the library collection. The Friends were really keen to ensure that the book collection retain the name the Whitfield Library, honouring a stalwart member who had been instrumental in its founding. At the Institute, there was a desire to name the room after first Secretary, Thomas MacNay, after whom the street leading to the Darlington Head of Steam Museum was also named. An agreeable compromise was reached, with the book collection becoming the Whitfield Library hosted in the MacNay Room. The books were transferred to their new home and a process of cataloguing commenced.

Above: The freshly redecorated MacNay Room, a formerly disused space at the Institute brought back into use hosting the Whitfield Library and meeting room for small community groups.

A 'library unveiling' event was planned and held on Saturday 4 March 2023, which highly appropriately coincided with the launch of a new book about Timothy Hackworth written by the York based author Mike Norman. Entitled "It Wasn't Rocket Science," this book builds a compelling case for looking again at Timothy Hackworth's influence in the development of the steam locomotive. It examines events of the early years on the Stockton and Darlington Railway, and the subsequent Rainhill Trials. The latter was a competition held in October 1829 to determine which rail engineer was best suited to be engaged to provide sufficiently powerful locomotives for the Liverpool and Manchester Railway.

In that contest, Hackworth's famous "Sans Pareil" was entered to compete against four other locomotives; Thomas Brandreth's "Cycloped," which was disqualified due to being powered by horse rather than steam, Timothy Burstall's "Perseverance", the "Rocket" built by the Stephensons and another engine named "Novelty" built by John Ericsson and John Braithwaite.

Above: Author, Mike Norman (right), presents Dave Reynolds and Jane Hackworth-Young a copy of his new book, championing Timothy Hackworth, for the reinstated Institute Library

Mike Norman's book launch event was very well attended, and afforded him the opportunity to present an excellent and informative speech on the argument for Hackworth's engineering contribution having being grossly understated by most experts across the decades.

Afterwards, several attendees retired to the MacNay Room to admire its redecoration and the revived Whitfield Library collection. Mike immediately donated a copy of his own book. Several further generous donations followed in the months since, and we anticipate that this may continue as we look to develop this special collection of useful knowledge and visual material, old and new, to make it available for our community in the future.

Reconstitution

From the beginning of the Institute's twenty-first century revival in 2019 the Institute and its volunteer partners from the Shildon Heritage Alliance CIC had been exploring a plan to reimagine a sustainable future for the Institute building. It was very apparent that maintenance of the building had been neglected since the handover from the British Rail Staff Association to the membership, and that the essential fabric of the building was by this point over a hundred years old.

The Institute committee were aware of some of the problems, as each year the winter weather was battering the building, causing new problems to resolve and necessitating essential repairs to stop existing problems worsening. Each repair added additional pressure to the Institute's ailing finances. No sooner was a small reserve of money established, than it was consumed again patching up part of the roof. On one occasion during the covid pandemic for example, a heavy snowfall settled on the roof of the Institute. As the snow melted some of the water leaked in through a breach in the roof above the stage in the main hall. This subsequently soaked into, and softened, the plaster ceiling above the stage which then collapsed onto it. Had the country not been subject to a Government enforced 'lock-down' this catastrophe would have resulted in cancellation of events and parties. This was repaired while the building was under enforced closure and very few members were ever aware of it happening.

Concerned about the overall state of the building, the Shildon Heritage Alliance CIC commissioned an initial condition survey through Eddisons surveyors. The report confirmed what had been feared, which was that aspects of the material fabric of the building were reaching the end of their serviceable life, and that the building would require renovation soon. The following extract from the executive summary in the report, produced on 5 May 2020, relates some of the most worrying factors.

> The second floor is in a significantly dilapidated condition from both a building fabric and health and safety perspective, with large openings noted to floors in numerous locations. Severe weathering / water ingress has led to structural damage to the dormer window above the stairwell (to the rear of the building), and this should be attended to immediately to avoid potential collapse of the dormer window.

The roofs to the original building comprise predominantly of dual-pitch roof construction with a Welsh slate finish, supported by timber roof joists which span from load-bearing walls up to a central timber ridge beam. In addition to the pitch roof construction, there are smaller sections of flat roof coverings; including over the Resident Steward's accommodation and rear offshoots.

The roof to the original building comprises a natural slate (Welsh) finish which is back pointed to the rafters with no breathable membrane present and is showing signs of significant delamination and discolouration. Without a breathable membrane to the roof build up, this can cause conditions which are conducive to timber rot and infestation, albeit there was no evidence of such defects noted. Internally, throughout the building, there were signs of significant water ingress affecting ceilings and walls as a result of the failure of the roof tiles. Furthermore, where inspected the roof access point to the second floor, there were various areas of clear daylight present which indicates that slates have also slipped as a result of nail corrosion (nail sickness).

We would recommend that these coverings are replaced in the short term, as the slates are now at the end of their expected design life (circa 100 years for Welsh slate). Our recommendation is on the basis that any further deterioration of the slate finish, inclusive of nail sickness, could lead to further slipped and misaligned tiles, subsequently allowing an increased amount of water ingress into the roof structure. If not attended to, the consequence is that the roof could continue to deteriorate and allow increased levels of water

This was alarming, though not unexpected, news. The surveyors estimated that, though there was no immediate safety danger, £2.27 million would need to be spent on a full building restoration project to place it in a condition in which it would be fit to keep serving its community for decades ahead. This was sobering news for a community organisation that generally carried less than half a percent of that amount as financial balance.

What on earth could be done? Here were the members of the Institute, its committee and volunteers, now custodians of one of the last living legacies of the world famous Stockton & Darlington Railway, one of the most significant industrial cultural buildings in the country, if not the world, facing this immense challenge to keep it from crumbling and eventual demolition.

Throughout Shildon's booming railway industry years, the first step would have been, of course, to begin by petitioning influential figures at whichever railway company was acting as the current patron. The industry would have undoubtedly realised the importance of offering some support given the Institute's status as a world first. In this third decade of the twenty-first century though, that industry has long since been dismantled by Government and replaced by a network of private companies, largely under foreign ownership and focused solely on extraction of profit. Other than being situated on one of the country's network of surviving branch lines, and the town hosting a branch of the Science Museum, this small place, the cradle of the steam hauled passenger railway, is no longer of interest or significance to what remains of the railway industry.

What then of the charitable trusts and bodies set up to look after heritage assets that had played a significant part in Britain's railway story? Surely they would take an interest in assuring the future of the world's first Institute set up for workers in the railway industry? Tentative queries quickly revealed that this was not the case. Bodies such as the Railway Heritage Trust limit the scope of their interest to buildings and estate that are or were part of the operational railway network, rather than the supporting social infrastructure. Had the Institute at Shildon been a listed station, signal box or notable engine shed, then its plight might have been of more interest to such organisations.

Enquiries as to what help might be available that were directed to the area's senior political figures bore little fruit, as most failed to see beyond the surface appearance of yet another ailing social club. They failed to grasp the significance the Institute held in the community, or its potential to be more than its current self. Some believed the sole concern to be the loss of the building rather than the combination of the building and the organisation that inhabits it. Unhelpful suggestions were made that the building might be sold to a private business that might find a sufficient use for it to want to then maintain it.

There was some hope and inspiration to be found in the form of initiatives that had been carried out elsewhere in the region on other buildings of industrial significance. In Durham, for example, a team had been working very hard making the case for renovation of the Durham Miners Hall at Redhills, better known as the Pitmen's Parliament, for its role as the headquarters of the Durham Miner's Association. When contacted for an exchange of information, the team there certainly saw a degree of similarity in the jeopardy faced by the Shildon Institute. There were other examples across the region where older significant buildings at the heart of communities had been saved by determined groups reaching out for the support of major funding partners, such as the National Lottery Community Fund or Heritage Fund. This was a possibility to be investigated with some urgency.

Initial tentative expressions of interest were submitted to a number of these bodies, some of whom offered the opportunity to have a discussion to understand how viable an application might be. Whilst the contacts from the funding bodies were both interested and sympathetic, some blocking factors were exposed.

Firstly, that the Shildon Heritage Alliance CIC, despite being a potentially fundable body registered with Companies House, would not be able to make any applications on behalf of the Institute. The Institute building belonged to the members and as such that organisation would have to apply for its own funding support. Secondly, the Institute as an organisation was not in a state of readiness for that process.

These bodies and other major funding partners place a number of conditions and qualifying criteria on organisations that can apply to them for financial help. These in turn are designed to protect the money that those parties are empowered to distribute, and ensure that it is genuinely employed to benefit communities. One of the main tests of an organisation's eligibility to apply is its legal status, and type of organisation. Organisations that are registered as having a charitable or community purpose, and that are consequently regulated as such, are held as being far more trustworthy than those that are not. This would not have struck the committee of the Institute as being important back in the mid 1980s when it was last re-constituted, and when the building was in much better health. Consequently, they had constituted the newly independent Institute as one of the least formal unregistered types of member organisations, nowadays known as an 'unincorporated association', placing it in a weak position to ask for help.

It appeared clear that whilst not changing its fundamental nature, the services the members valued, or its purpose, the Institute would need to convert to a new form of legal entity in order to fight on for a continued future. Furthermore, with competition for available funding being fierce, it would be necessary to learn how to be effective at applying for funding applications with such large funding partners.

The volunteers from the Shildon Heritage Alliance CIC enrolled on a one year part time Heritage Compass course while the Institute sought guidance from Durham Community Action, another organisation established to support community organisations in these situations. The Heritage Compass course set out how to establish good organisational governance, develop an audience for your services, develop a business plan, how to manage and plan finances to demonstrate proven sustainability, to engage in marketing, to diversify what you offer to deliver the greatest community benefit and importantly what the funders look for when considering major funding applications. In parallel to this, other volunteers and the Committee received guidance on types of legal entity, the pros and cons of each, and which might prove the best fit for Shildon Railway Institute. This included an amount of free advice from a Solicitor with expertise on the subject.

It was going to be very important to find a type of organisation that would still leave the Institute true to its original purpose, that it would still be self contained and member owned, that would be led by a committee of members elected from the body of the membership and would be able to offer the services valued by the members. This process of consultation ruled out options that replaced the committee with boards of directors or trustees. The conclusion was that the best fit might be to become a Community Benefit Society, a relatively new organisational format that had been enabled under the Co-operative and Community Benefit Societies Act of 2014. Furthermore, advice was given that key funding providers had been contacted and had confirmed that this was among their favoured business models.

What would Shildon Railway Institute look like as a Community Benefit Society, and would the membership agree to the change? A meeting of the committee was held in December 2022 and permission was given to form a Transformation Steering Committee to explore that question and to formulate a proposal to present to members. This Steering Committee, a panel of Institute committee, volunteers and regular members met every Saturday from the first week of 2023, researching what was necessary to be done, scrutinising model rules, assessing the fit for the Institute and creating the draft policies that were prerequisite to being accepted as a Community Benefit Society.

The process of formulation of a proposal was kept as transparent as possible throughout with minutes of the weekly meetings being posted online and on the Institute notice board.

In mid-May the Steering Committee announced their intention to hold a meeting of all members on Sunday 4 June at which the proposal would be presented to the members for consideration. Posters declaring that "It's Time To Decide" were pinned up and posted online. The design depicted a pocket watch, a cryptic reference to that incident that caused the Institute to be formed back in 1833, in which George Graham, traffic manager of the Stockton and Darlington Railway had encountered locomotive drivers throwing their pocket watches into a frying pan and betting on which would stop first.

A large number of members attended the meeting at which a twenty minute video explaining the rationale was screened, and members were then given the opportunity to ask questions or share thoughts. The documents making up the proposal had been made available two weeks in advance for members to examine and query. That meeting also marked the beginning of a week long period in which members could collect their ballot paper and cast their vote on whether each supported or opposed the proposal to convert the Institute to become a Community Benefit Society, and in doing so to adopt the new proposed rules of the Institute.

Above: Members attend a video presentation in the Institute's main hall, on proposals to transform the legal format of the Institute to a Community Benefit Society.

The ballot closed at 4pm on Sunday 11 June 2023 and the ballot box unlocked. At 5:00pm a count of votes was conducted under the watchful eye of an appointed independent scrutiniser, Professor Alan Townsend, of the Friends of the Stockton and Darlington Railway. Additional votes had been received electronically through an online process, designed to enable votes of members who were no longer locally resident. These were validated and checked to ensure there were no duplicates votes.

At the conclusion of the count, the Institute Secretary,

Shaun Thompson, took the floor to declare that though there had been 2 votes against the proposal, there had been 200 votes for it, and that therefore the balloted motion was passed. Shildon Railway Institute would take the initial steps to become a Community Benefit Society. The 200 votes counted represented a view of more than half of the registered membership at that time.

Above: Prof. Alan Townsend acts as independent scrutineer as the ballot on the proposal to reconstitute the Institute as a Community Benefit Society is counted.

In thanking the members present for their active participation in this decision making process, the Chair of the Steering Committee, Dave Reynolds added that he felt that becoming a Community Benefit Society was not in itself "a magic wand, but it was at least a ticket to get to meet the Fairy Godmother." By this he meant that once the registration of the Community Benefit Society was complete the Institute would be able to talk to funders, apply for funding and be taken seriously.

A future for the Institute was still going to be challenging, and as if circumstances weren't difficult enough already the whole country was in the grip of what had been termed a national 'cost of living' crisis. In February 2022, Russia had invaded the neighbouring country of Ukraine, to global condemnation. In a related response to the reaction of western nations to this invasion Russian gas companies cut off supply to Europe creating an energy shortage, and triggering severe price rises throughout the year. Energy companies protected their businesses by increasing the price of gas and electricity to homes and businesses, the Institute among them. Here, the electricity bills doubled and price of gas per unit increased fivefold. There was an accompanying inflationary spiral that saw the cost of absolutely everything the Institute needed to operate rising.

Suddenly, the challenge of Covid lockdowns seemed like a distant memory, and the future far less certain. As each crippling energy bill landed on the Secretary's desk, the Institute seemed to be creeping closer to the edge of a precipice and there were worries that the next might prove to be the un-payable one that might trigger the Institute's end.

As the spring came to an end bringing warmer summer weather, there was a temporary sigh of relief at the understanding that the Institute had for now avoided financial collapse only by the skin of its teeth. Another such winter, if longer or harder, might not be survivable. For a while the Committee diverted away from the transition to concentrate on building back a financial reserve and considering alternative approaches to gas for heating the building in winter in future. Generous members rallied, donating amounts large and small to help build back some financial resilience.

Marking 190 Years

At the beginning of 2023 there was a recognition that the year ahead would bring the 190th Anniversary of the founding of the railway institute. Given how tough the past five years had been it seemed like a milestone that the Institute ought to be celebrating. An opportunity to take stock, and to charge the enthusiasm of the membership to look ahead to the next ten years which, if successful, would lead us to bicentenary plans for 2033. It was an opportunity to focus on charting a course toward that goal.

Suggestions were made as to what might make up a reasonable, and affordable, programme of activities to raise awareness of our having achieved the significant milestone of nineteen unbroken decades in the service of our community, and a shortlist of six possibilities was drawn up from which four were pursued.

The first goal was to launch the reborn Institute library, which we discussed in a previous chapter. The second idea was to create something that the members could keep. It was decided that a limited run of three-hundred Institute 190th Anniversary badges should be created and made available. The design for this was created by one of the volunteers and featured a locomotive wheel in the North Eastern Railway green on a black and gold background with the number 190 in white at front and centre. This design was also produced on special celebratory beer mats that could be used throughout the year. A third goal was to produce this book, that you hold in your hands right now, telling the story of our journey from a handful of determined men in the cellar of a long demolished public house to where we are today, and as much as we could about what happened along the way. The final goal was to hold a grand celebratory event as close as practicably possible to the actual anniversary date of 28 November 2023.

Two ideas that were ultimately discarded, were eliminated only on the grounds of not having the capacity to do everything whilst attending to the day-to-day problems of keeping the Institute in business. One of these was to have had a 190th Anniversary weekend of sports and games with what is now the BR Sports & Social Club, which after all was a spin-off of the original Institute and only separated as a consequence of that parting of ways in the mid-nineteen-eighties when the British Rail Staff Association was disposing of social assets. Though the 'BR', as the sports club it is affectionately known, may have felt like a separate thing since the ground was opened in 1955, its roots are common with the Institute. The idea was abandoned after tentative contact between the two associations as it was proving difficult to get volunteer 'captains' to co-ordinate teams for the Institute, and the committee didn't have the capacity at the time to take more on. The final idea, which also ultimately didn't progress, was a "Steam at the Stute" family day which would have seen a display of steam static and traction engines on the Institute's land to the rear of the main building. Again there were concerns over having the capacity to promote and run the event properly and safely, and the suitability of the land for it given its current state. Both of these were deemed ideas that could be returned to in the future.

The idea for the 190th Anniversary Gala Concert had been inspired by the fundraising online variety concert that had been held for the Institute's 187th anniversary during the Covid-19 lockdown. Though the upcoming event was not intended to be a fund-raiser, it was felt that the variety element, showcasing different acts, was both a good way to offer something for everyone and also very similar in format to some of the events held at the Institute in the past and for which the Institute still held posters in its collection. In those bygone days the evening would generally be centred around a dance band with a variety of singers. For this event it was thought that it would be fitting to invite back some music artists that had become good friends of the Institute in recent years.

Above: The special limited edition enamelled metal 190th anniversary pin badge in black, white, green and gold

The first of these was Sam Slatcher of Citizen Songwriters. It was felt that to start the evening with his co-created songs about the town and local area would be a fitting way to enter into the evening in the right spirit. It was after all an evening about celebrating ourselves as a community as much as it was about enjoying ourselves.

The second performer to take the stage was chosen not only for being a talent capable of entertaining a room full of people, but also because she was 'one of our own'. Steph Austin is a member of the Institute, daughter of a long standing former treasurer, Ricky Wilkinson, but also an employee at the Institute. She began her career as a singer with a performance at the Institute and is much loved by many of the members there. It simply felt as though the night would be incomplete without her bringing her smooth vocal style and quirky amiable manner to the party.

A third performer on the bill was another great local talent, Richie Boddy, who had up until that point been more commonly associated through his appearances with highly popular sixties covers band The Fabs, but whom we knew to be a more than capable performer and entertainer in his own right. His stripped back renditions of songs, accompanied only by acoustic guitar and a bass drum, highlighted his mastery of the instrument and versatile rangy vocal style.

The final act bringing the 190th Anniversary concert to a rousing close, were the local Irish folk quartet, The Shamrocks, who had been making an appearance in one form or another, individually or together annually at the Institute for around four years. It was known that they could be relied upon to make the finale of the evening feel like a true celebration, and they did not disappoint.

The main hall at the Institute had been dressed for the evening in the 190th Anniversary themed colours of green, black and gold - with tables covered in cloths of these colours with gold streamers strewn across them. Bunting was hung from the ceiling and walls and clusters of helium filled balloons hung suspended in the air.

As a centrepiece for the event, a magnificent cake had been created for the event, through the kind generosity of Jayne Todd, a member of the Institute whose late father Terry Fuller had served on the committee, and whom with his wife Ann had long been committed supporters of the organisation. Jayne's 190th Anniversary cake was a replica of the Institute's current Redworth Road building in miniature, and constructed from sponge cake with buttercream filling coated with fondant icing. Every pane of the windows, every door, even the flower planters on the forecourt that volunteers fill with flowering plants each year; all were represented in this impressive baked masterpiece which drew admiration from onlookers throughout the evening.

Whilst the evening might not have been the grandest party ever held by the Institute; and it may have lacked the stags heads, heraldic imagery, technical drawings and festoons of greenery that decorated those tea parties back when Timothy Hackworth presided over affairs, it certainly felt like a celebration, and one that would live long in the memory of those that attended. There is really so much to be proud of, and so much worthy of celebrating, even today. Perhaps it might have even whet appetites for what might be achieved if we are successful in reaching our bicentenary in 2033. How grand a celebration we might create for that milestone?

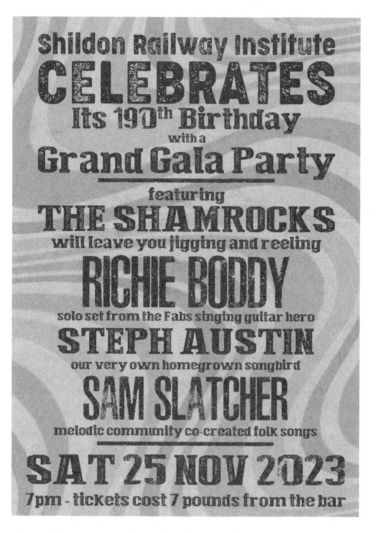

Above: The 'retro' poster design created to promote the Institute's 190th Anniversary Grand Gala Party in November 2023

Looking Ahead Up The Line

Thus our journey through one-hundred-and-ninety years of this organisation draws to its conclusion, for now. And it has indeed been like a journey by train, for as you might look out of a window as you race through the countryside you may notice many sights and scenes, but in doing so there are others that slip by unnoticed while you admired the ones that caught our attention. Our history of the Institute is alas very like that. For everything we have recalled here there will be tens of others that we were unable to include. Significant people that have played a part at every step along the way; fathers, mothers, aunts and uncles, grandfathers and great grandfathers. Each one of them having played a part in making the Institute a special place that creates fondness for this old society for so many today. So many memories of parties past, outings enjoyed, capers and japes, personal triumphs and tragedies.

There are so many people unnamed here, to whom a debt is owed. The visionaries, organisers, practical people, fundraisers, entertainers, hard-working servants, promotors, volunteers, heroes of games and sports, optimists, enthusiasts and critics. Every one of them deserves a page here and their omission is not a deliberate sleight so much as an admission that to cover their individual contributions would be a task without end.

Before looking ahead we pause momentarily to tale a look brief look around us at 'The Stute' today. Entering the building through the double doors beneath the misdated keystone of the entrance arch, we find ourselves in a brightly lit entrance hallway. To our left we see the Shildon Works as it would have appeared when the building was but young. Ahead of us, the main stairway winds its way up to the first floor. First though, we go to the right, into the main hall. Here on Mondays you might join the weekly dancercise class, to keep fit in a fun way, or wait until a Tuesday where you might join the older traditional grace of the modern sequence dancers. Halloween and Christmas bring the delighted shrieks of children's parties. Much has changed since the hall hosted Vincent Raven and Arthur Pease on opening day. A recessed stage suitable for entertainments has replaced the speakers lecture platform. The barrelled ceiling lowered around the edges to bring cosiness and arched skylight covered. Windows that once let light in on both sides have been boarded to make the hall perfect for party lights all year round. The timbered centre ceiling still reverberates the echoes of so many parties past and present.

Leaving the hall and crossing to the lounge, named in honour of founder and first President, we enter to find the walls adorned with photographs of the building as it was when it opened, and the silver key that was used on that opening day. Timothy Hackworth himself, depicted as a young man, looks down upon us from his frame. To the left of him two images of his innovative Sans Pareil locomotive. Here on Sundays and Wednesdays, silence descends for Bingo, or on Sunday afternoons the fragrances of hot dogs, onions and sauce fill the area as Shildon Institute FC take a well deserved post-match rest to reflect on the week's result. Monthly you might try your knowledge in a music or general knowledge quiz, join in a British Legion branch social or chat over achievements with fellows from a club or society.

Above: The main hall being decked and draped ready for a royal celebration doesn't deter this determined dancercise class.

Following the passage along to the bar, we step into the beating heart of the building as it now is. It appears a little tired, but with good reason, for it has been well enjoyed. Look around and you will see the giant images on the Shildon Works suspended upon the walls; montages of smiling snapshots from celebrations past, a royal wedding or a jubilee and group portraits of the Touring

Club from bygone years. It's a pace in which to reflect upon the trials, tribulations and triumphs of those long, or recently, gone before us, and revel in the real world company of those in here in the now. Close your eyes and listen for the pop and crack of a skilled pool player making their opening break in a Wednesday night league match, or the gentle thunk, thunk, thunk of tungsten in the sisal surface of the darts board. Here within this room every conversation imaginable has been held and many a world 'put to rights' before eleven o'clock, in words if not in deeds. It is a well loved place to meet at the end of any day, but Sunday afternoon is when it crackles most vibrantly with life. At such times the chattering and murmuring of voices, male and female, swells punctuated by the swoosh and swirl of tiles on board as opponents vie to be crowned domino champion of the day. News and opinions are exchanged, and tall tales traded for ill remembered jokes. Domino cards and raffle tickets are passed around by stout hearted and vital volunteers in the knowledge that participation enables good things, as well as the outside chance of a prize. And all of this is enabled, supervised and facilitated by a kind and patient small crew of staff, in their Railway Institute polo shirts, unfalteringly loyal to place, members and to each other.

This is what the Institute is today, a coming together of people bound together through a common geography. Some will tell you of their family ties; the unbroken presence of generations past within the bounds of the three wards that make up the town. They will tell you how they cannot see themselves anywhere else in the world. Others give themselves away as incomers through their tell-tale accents; a Scottish burr, the dropped 'h' of a southern accent, or the broad dialect of a Geordie or "sand-dancer". At times the sound of voices from beyond our nation's borders, to east or west, joins the clamour Yet there is no hierarchy here. The new roots and tendrils of place and belonging are quickly cultivated within these walls.

The Institute today is a tonic for loneliness, a place where you become embraced by a wider family if you wish to be, or can sit back, observe and absorb if you do not. For those that have not chosen, or lack the means to afford, withdrawal into the cosy numbness of a digital escape existence into a constantly pre-imagined curated and cultivated world, the Institute is an environment from which the invasive modernity of superficial digital interaction retreats and diminishes. Real world conversations re-emerge, renewing old bonds, creating new friendships, cementing family ties. The angry capital letters and emphatic italics of social media posts screamed into a dark electronic void, that barely listens, give way to still strong but mainly respectful debate, the fallouts from which rarely last beyond the next trip to the bar. It may not be precisely what they directors of four successive railway companies had in mind, but in the present times, in which social and community cohesion is brittle, it is beyond determinable value.

Yet the world in which we live is changing, and often at a sometimes frightening pace that leaves many of us discomforted. So too are the needs and behaviours of the people that inhabit it. Just as the needs and desires of our forebears ceded making way for ours, we cannot assume that everything enjoyed at the Stute today will hold the same value for those to whom we might hand over this wonderful 'people powered' movement tomorrow. It will always be important to look back, to understand how and why this society was created. We can learn something from every generation that can help us in the present. Just as important is the need to look forward to the future. That capability to detect a navigable route toward possibilities of the future was a capability demonstrable by the people who founded 'the Stute'. They did not perceive at the outset what it might become, or who would steer it in new directions with each generation. Yet they created that opportunity, and invited people to be part of the process. Perhaps that is what we need to do next. Look to the present generation to work with the next to seek out a path toward a Stute as yet unknown. It feels important that while doing this we should still be looking after those needs of those who prepared the way for us.

As I write this, we appear to be a nation that has somehow lost its love of socialising person-to-person. In decades past, the time-honoured rituals of spending time together in shared spaces in groups seemed unassailable. It was, for many of us now over the age of forty, how friendships started, how bonds were formed and broken, how we discovered and explored love and how we formed our social identity. Now it appears that so many of us take every opportunity to retreat to the enclosed sanctuary of our homes. Rather than revel in the likelihood of a chance encounter with a prospective new partner, we advertise ourselves in a digital marketplace and coolly browse for compatible and viable partners that meet our exacting criteria. Instead of hunting for a seat with a view in a room with a hundred or so others watching whatever singer or band has been booked together, we opt to join the millions upon millions summoning precisely whatever we want to watch to the nearest screen. We find the risk of having to hold a conversation with someone else, someone who might see the world differently, so averse that we retreat to scroll through reams of more palatable opinions in the echo chambers of social media. Often, even though groups of us might be seen out together, we are only sharing a physical space and are otherwise captivated and transported to other places, and the company of other people more to our liking With the screens we carry wherever we go, many of us we are often together whilst, at the same time, very much apart.

Nobody at this time knows if the social drift we're seeing today is going to be permanent. Only if anyone reads this in decades to come might they know better. But if it is, what might the Institute of the future be like? Might its building continue to be a relevant place in which we will take time out to explore and celebrate the rich social, cultural and industrial heritage we have chosen to set aside? Might there be new societies or groups formed to take part in traditional pastimes? Or might it become a place in which our community can explore new and innovative ways to come together. New games or sports, or new digital innovations that require more space than our homes offer us.

Personally, I hope that whatever it becomes will be something that continues to put people and their contemporary needs at its heart. It should not seek to become a museum in which we simply admire the great people that first gave it momentum, or in which we might pine for the past. Reminders, and an understanding of, its past should always be present to help it focus on what's important for a meaningful future. By this I mean that if you look at a society that has constantly evolved only as what you see today, you might forget that evolution is not only possible, but natural and beneficial. Knowing how something has evolved might help us see how, and when, the next evolutionary stage is due.

Beyond everything I hope that the Stute, in whatever form it takes, endures so that those who are to come can enjoy its benefits as we do now, and as those who have gone before us did. It would be heartbreaking if it were to cease, or it's building to fall derelict.

That will only be possible if it continues to be valued, and if people rally to it, bringing whatever qualities and ideas they have to offer. At it has for 190 years now, the Stute will need people with vision, with determination and with skills. It will need volunteers, organisers, administrators, people with practical skills, people who are not afraid to have a go, or those who know they have something to offer even if they are not sure how helpful that might be. If you have read this and taken anything from it, I hope that it is the understanding that Shildon Railway Institute is not bricks and mortar. It has not always had a building to call its own. Nor is it simply a social-club. It is a movement of people, for people. It is a rallying point for a community in good times, bad times, and something always well worth playing a part in.

Shildon Railway Institute successfully registered as a reconstituted Community Benefit Society on 3 January 2024 - but still faces a battle for its future.

TO BE CONTINUED.

By the same author.

"The Wizard and The Typhoon"
(2022)

There is no sound that encapsulates the spirit of the industrial communities of the North East of England better than the music produced by a brass band.

Though Shildon's band-rooms have been silent for decades, it was the birthplace of two of the most influential and talented brass composers the world has seen. From childhood pals to competitive rivals and internationally known composers, the lives of George Allan and Tom Bulch could not have been more different, yet at the same time so alike.

The Wizard and The Typhoon chronicles their entwined story, from their births in the early 1860s to their deaths in 1930. It is set in a social history of the glories of the Victorian era through to the technological revolutions of the early twentieth century, and encapsulates their great triumphs and profound tragedies.

It is a true story of two remarkable Shildon men, their families and their friends on the world stage, and how even though they are long gone, their influence still reverberates today.

available from Amazon.co.uk

Printed in Great Britain
by Amazon

40375096R00119